| Cults

Other Books of Related Interest:

Opposing Viewpoints Series

Church and State

Doomsday Scenarios

Human Rights

Militias

At Issue Series

Do Children Have Rights?

How Does Religion Influence Politics?

Polygamy

Should Religious Symbols Be Allowed on Public Land?

Current Controversies Series

Assisted Suicide

Family Violence

Human Trafficking

Islamophobia

"Congress shall make no law . . . abridging the freedom of speech, or of the press."

First Amendment to the US Constitution

The basic foundation of our democracy is the First Amendment guarantee of freedom of expression. The Opposing Viewpoints series is dedicated to the concept of this basic freedom and the idea that it is more important to practice it than to enshrine it.

OPPOSING VIEWPOINTS® SERIES

I Cults

Roman Espejo, Book Editor

GREENHAVEN PRESS
A part of Gale, Cengage Learning

GALE
CENGAGE Learning·

Detroit • New York • San Francisco • New Haven, Conn • Waterville, Maine • London

Elizabeth Des Chenes, *Director, Publishing Solutions*

© 2013 Greenhaven Press, a part of Gale, Cengage Learning.

Gale and Greenhaven Press are registered trademarks used herein under license.

For more information, contact:
Greenhaven Press
27500 Drake Rd.
Farmington Hills, MI 48331-3535
Or you can visit our Internet site at gale.cengage.com

For product information and technology assistance, contact us at

Gale Customer Support, 1-800-877-4253
For permission to use material from this text or product, submit all requests online at
www.cengage.com/permissions

Further permissions questions can be emailed to permissionrequest@cengage.com

Articles in Greenhaven Press anthologies are often edited for length to meet page requirements. In addition, original titles of these works are changed to clearly present the main thesis and to explicitly indicate the author's opinion. Every effort is made to ensure that Greenhaven Press accurately reflects the original intent of the authors. Every effort has been made to trace the owners of copyrighted material.

Cover Image copyright © cdsk/www.fotosearch.com. Stock Photography.

LIBRARY OF CONGRESS CATALOGING-IN-PUBLICATION DATA

Cults / Roman Espejo, book editor.
p. cm. -- (Opposing viewpoints)
Includes bibliographical references and index.
ISBN 978-0-7377-3994-7 (hardcover) -- ISBN 978-0-7377-3995-4 (pbk.)
1. Cults. I. Espejo, Roman, 1977-
BP603.C846 2012
200--dc23

2012013293

Printed in the United States of America
1 2 3 4 5 6 7 16 15 14 13 12

Contents

Why Consider Opposing Viewpoints?

"The only way in which a human being can make some approach to knowing the whole of a subject is by hearing what can be said about it by persons of every variety of opinion and studying all modes in which it can be looked at by every character of mind. No wise man ever acquired his wisdom in any mode but this."

John Stuart Mill

In our media-intensive culture it is not difficult to find differing opinions. Thousands of newspapers and magazines and dozens of radio and television talk shows resound with differing points of view. The difficulty lies in deciding which opinion to agree with and which "experts" seem the most credible. The more inundated we become with differing opinions and claims, the more essential it is to hone critical reading and thinking skills to evaluate these ideas. Opposing Viewpoints books address this problem directly by presenting stimulating debates that can be used to enhance and teach these skills. The varied opinions contained in each book examine many different aspects of a single issue. While examining these conveniently edited opposing views, readers can develop critical thinking skills such as the ability to compare and contrast authors' credibility, facts, argumentation styles, use of persuasive techniques, and other stylistic tools. In short, the Opposing Viewpoints series is an ideal way to attain the higher-level thinking and reading skills so essential in a culture of diverse and contradictory opinions.

In addition to providing a tool for critical thinking, Opposing Viewpoints books challenge readers to question their own strongly held opinions and assumptions. Most people form their opinions on the basis of upbringing, peer pressure, and personal, cultural, or professional bias. By reading carefully balanced opposing views, readers must directly confront new ideas as well as the opinions of those with whom they disagree. This is not to argue simplistically that everyone who reads opposing views will—or should—change his or her opinion. Instead, the series enhances readers' understanding of their own views by encouraging confrontation with opposing ideas. Careful examination of others' views can lead to the readers' understanding of the logical inconsistencies in their own opinions, perspective on why they hold an opinion, and the consideration of the possibility that their opinion requires further evaluation.

Evaluating Other Opinions

To ensure that this type of examination occurs, Opposing Viewpoints books present all types of opinions. Prominent spokespeople on different sides of each issue as well as well-known professionals from many disciplines challenge the reader. An additional goal of the series is to provide a forum for other, less known, or even unpopular viewpoints. The opinion of an ordinary person who has had to make the decision to cut off life support from a terminally ill relative, for example, may be just as valuable and provide just as much insight as a medical ethicist's professional opinion. The editors have two additional purposes in including these less known views. One, the editors encourage readers to respect others' opinions—even when not enhanced by professional credibility. It is only by reading or listening to and objectively evaluating others' ideas that one can determine whether they are worthy of consideration. Two, the inclusion of such viewpoints encourages the important critical thinking skill of objectively evaluating an author's credentials and bias. This evaluation will illuminate an author's reasons for taking a particular stance on an issue and will aid in readers' evaluation of the author's ideas.

It is our hope that these books will give readers a deeper understanding of the issues debated and an appreciation of the complexity of even seemingly simple issues when good and honest people disagree. This awareness is particularly important in a democratic society such as ours in which people enter into public debate to determine the common good. Those with whom one disagrees should not be regarded as enemies but rather as people whose views deserve careful examination and may shed light on one's own.

Thomas Jefferson once said that "difference of opinion leads to inquiry, and inquiry to truth." Jefferson, a broadly educated man, argued that "if a nation expects to be ignorant and free . . . it expects what never was and never will be." As individuals and as a nation, it is imperative that we consider the opinions of others and examine them with skill and discernment. The Opposing Viewpoints series is intended to help readers achieve this goal.

David L. Bender and Bruno Leone,
Founders

Introduction

> "There are plenty of millennial cults who are preparing themselves for the end of the world."
>
> —Nigel Cawthorne,
> author of Doomsday:
> 50 Visions of the End of the World

> "It is important to realize that out of the tens of thousands of new religious groups worldwide, only a very few meet these criteria [of doomsday cults]."
>
> —Bruce A. Robinson,
> founder of Ontario Consultants
> on Religious Tolerance

In 2011 a doomsday prediction made headlines around the world. Christian evangelist Harold Camping, then president of the California-based Family Radio, had proclaimed that Judgment Day would occur on May 21. According to him, Jesus Christ would return on that exact date, and righteous Christian believers would ascend to heaven, leaving the rest of the world to perish in a massive earthquake. Plagues, fire, and brimstone would follow for the next five months—causing millions of deaths each day—until Armageddon on October 21.

In the months preceding May 21, Family Radio mounted an international billboard campaign for Judgment Day; two thousand signs popped up overseas as far as Russia, Lebanon, and Dubai. Many of Camping's followers quit their jobs and poured their life savings and efforts into spreading the word. "I'm trying to warn people about what's coming,"[1] said Rob-

1. *New York Daily News*, May 12, 2011. http://articles.nydailynews.com.

ert Fitzpatrick, a retiree who spent $140,000 to advertise Family Radio's message in the mass transit system of New York City. "People who have an understanding," he explained, "have an obligation to warn everyone."

When the events that Camping prophesized did not occur, he then explained that his followers had been spiritually judged on that day, and the apocalypse would begin on October 21. After that failed prediction, Camping retired from Family Radio and, in private, admitted that no one could know when the world would end. The congregation of Family Radio has shrunken considerably; however, despite the spectacular failure, some followers remain. "A few people might abandon the group, typically the newest or least-committed adherents, but the vast majority experience little cognitive dissonance and so make only minor adjustments to their beliefs,"[2] explains Vaughan Bell, a clinical and neuropsychologist, about this behavior. "They carry on, often feeling more spiritually enriched as a result."

Some critics label Harold Camping and his followers as a doomsday cult, a destructive religious or spiritual group that revolves around or attempts to bring about the apocalypse. Glenn Hendrickson, a graduate student at Golden Gate Baptist Theological Seminary and blogger on religion, maintained that Family Radio should have taken the following actions after May 21: "Repent of being a cult and guessing (wrongly) when Jesus would return"[3] and "issue an apology to the world." It is also warned that the organization's apocalyptic teachings are harmful because they can promote irrational actions and decisions. "What troubles me is the 'all in' fervor of those who follow people like him,"[4] claims John Vest, a Presbyterian pastor and biblical scholar. "The kind of fundamentalism practiced and promoted by Camping is less deadly but

2. *Slate*, May 20, 2011. www.slate.com.
3. *The Apologist*, May 22, 2011. http://eyeonapologetics.com.
4. Johnvest.com, May 23, 2011. http://johnvest.com.

is no less problematic than the kind of fundamentalism that encourages believers to take their own lives and/or the lives of others," he argues.

Nonetheless, other commentators resist portraying Family Radio as a doomsday cult, explaining that Camping's prophecy was the result of an erroneous, but not malicious, interpretation of the Bible. "I do not believe that Harold Camping is a crackpot or a cult leader, though some will construe him as such. I believe that he got caught up in a particular way of looking at the Scriptures, and was eventually surrounded by people who believed likewise,"[5] alleges Timothy Dalrymple, managing editor of *Evangelical Portal*. Indeed, Dalrymple places accountability on Camping's believers for not questioning his claims and failing to listen to the skeptical voices around them. "His followers should also have been more critical, quicker to test him, and less quick to explain away the inconsistencies. They also should have listened to the gentle criticisms and encouragements they received from fellow believers who did not accept the May 21st prophecy," he insists. Others defend the evangelist's choice to raise awareness of his prediction, however polarizing or radical. "How many other Christian preachers do you see who truly believe in their faith enough to put it uncompromisingly in harm's way, the way Camping did?"[6] asks Deacon Duncan, author of *After Jesus Dies*. He purports that Christians throughout history have kept their prophecies "vague" to prevent their doctrines from being scrutinized as true or false. "He took Christianity seriously," argues Duncan, "and that was his downfall."

Whether or not a cult, Family Radio and its highly publicized and ridiculed campaign for Judgment Day renewed attention to such groups. *Opposing Viewpoints: Cults* investigates the characteristics, beliefs, methods, and behaviors of these organizations—as well as their leaders and followers—in the fol-

5. *Philosophical Fragments*, May 21, 2011. www.patheos.com.
6. *Evangelical Realism*, May 23, 2005. http://realevang.wordpress.com.

lowing chapters: What Are Cults?, Are Cults a Serious Threat?, Why Do People Join Cults?, and How Can Cult Members Be Helped? The varying explanations, arguments, and narratives offered in this anthology are a testament to cults as a controversial social, psychological, and spiritual phenomenon.

OPPOSING
VIEWPOINTS®
SERIES

I What Are Cults?

Chapter Preface

Founded in the 1870s by a Pennsylvania Bible study group, Jehovah's Witnesses has grown to 7.5 million followers worldwide, with almost 300,000 newly baptized members in 2010. Witnesses are known for their "person-to-person ministry," preaching door-to-door and in public places. "Following the model of first-century Christianity, Jehovah's Witnesses have no clergy-laity division. All baptized members are ordained ministers and share in the preaching and teaching work," the group states. Its journals, *The Watchtower Announcing Jehovah's Kingdom* and *Awake!*, are the first and second most widely distributed publications on the planet; in total, more than eighty million copies are printed each month.

The beliefs of Jehovah's Witnesses are based on its translation of the Bible that is known as *New World Translation of the Holy Scriptures*. The group predicts Armageddon, or "the war of the great day of God the Almighty," wherein "right-hearted individuals, wherever they may be on earth, will be preserved," and denies the soul's immortality, existence of hell, and the Holy Trinity. Witnesses also do not observe Christmas, Easter, or other holidays and traditions, associating them with paganism. "Jesus never commanded Christians to celebrate his birth. Rather, he told his disciples to memorialize, or remember, his death," the group declares. In addition, Witnesses do not celebrate birthdays and prohibit blood transfusions and military service.

Because of these aspects, some label Jehovah's Witnesses as a cult. "Jehovah's Witnesses originally taught that the world would end in 1914. It obviously did not," insists evangelist Pat Robertson. "They also taught that there were only 144,000 people who were going to be saved by going to heaven. When Jehovah's Witnesses membership went past 144,000, they said they were the meek and were going to inherit the earth," he adds. Others allege that Witnesses are under authoritarian control. "Once I left the group and did a lot of research on thought reform and mind control, however, I realized that Jehovah's Witnesses are being psychologically held hostage *within a cult*," claims cult expert Brenda Lee. "The invisible chains that bound me as a former Jehovah's Witness were quite real from the ages of nine until eighteen," Lee says.

However, in the *Watchtower*, the group maintains it is dogged by misperceptions. "If it ever crossed your mind that Jehovah's Witnesses might be a secret cult or sect, that was likely because *you* knew too little about them," it contends. "Dedicated as they are to the open and public service of God, Jehovah's Witnesses will be happy to reveal the plain facts of their activity and beliefs to anyone who cares to know the facts." In the following chapter, the authors debate what separates cults and religions.

> "Cults limit lives into narrow, claustro-
> phobic existences whose singular pur-
> pose is the cult itself."

Cults Are Harmful and Extreme Religious Groups

Jayanti Tamm

Jayanti Tamm is the author of Cartwheels in a Sari: A Memoir
of Growing Up Cult *and a visiting professor at Queens College.
In the following viewpoint, she claims that cults are religious or
spiritual organizations that use oppressive, debasing tactics to
place members under absolute control. Cults do not announce
themselves, Tamm maintains, and employ recruiting techniques
that are deceptively benign and caring to lure and indoctrinate
members. She describes several signs of a cult, such as the group
and leader are always correct and justified; total dependency on
the group and leader for basic decision making; requirement of
monetary payment, sex, or servitude for advancement; and separation of an evil "outside" world and chosen "inside" group.*

As you read, consider the following questions:

1. How is the cult leader's personal agenda presented, as
described by Tamm?

Jayanti Tamm, "What Is A Cult? Recognizing and Avoiding Unhealthy Groups," *Huffing-
ton Post*, April 14, 2011. Reproduced by permission of the author.

2. How does Tamm characterize a cult leader?

3. How does the author respond to the perception that imbalanced and weak individuals join cults?

Who in our over-stimulated, media-saturated, hyper-connected world would ever go and knowingly join a cult? The answer is no one.

No one wakes up one morning and decides to join a cult. Even if someone did, good luck trying to look up the address for the nearest local cult, for there isn't a single group that would ever admit to or advertise as being a cult. And why would they? The word "cult" is explosive, loaded with connotations of brainwashing, lunatics and mass suicide—not exactly an ideal marketing strategy. For the most part, cults are keenly and obsessively aware of their public persona and consciously labor to maintain a positive image.

Scrolling through their websites, their mission statements are warmly fuzzy and vague; they promise redemption, renewal, rejuvenation and reinvention. They offer answers, solutions and happiness. It's all there, yours for the taking. What isn't included is the reality beneath the surface, the leader's demands for obedience from its members, the psychological pressure, the ability to subordinate all activities to the leader's will.

But most people don't find and join cults through Internet searches. Most people stumble upon them accidentally. A flyer in the Laundromat for a free meditation class. A listing in the newspaper for a community service project. A poster at the library for a musical performance. Recruitment is purposefully subtle; the pull is gentle, gradual. Events are welcoming; attention is lavished on the visitor with the intention to create an environment that feels inclusive, nonthreatening and safe. The visitor is warmly encouraged to return, to step in closer. It is not until later, often much later, that one may look around and, with great surprise, discover the strange terrain upon which one now stands.

Absolute and Unconditional Control

Cults, whether they are offshoots of Eastern or Western traditional religions, are surprisingly similar in their methods and means. The tactics and techniques used to recruit, maintain and disown noncompliant members seem pulled from a universal handbook of dos and don'ts. With all of their rules and restrictions, laws and codes, ultimately cults are about grasping and preserving absolute and unconditional control.

Cults are fueled by and thrive on control. The willingness to surrender control comes from excessive devotion to the leader and the leader's vision. The leader's personal agenda is presented as a universal elixir, one that will eradicate both personal and global moral, ethical and spiritual maladies. The follower's faith becomes both the provider and the enabler.

Faith in the mission, faith in the leader is an agent used to unify a disparate collection of strong individuals from different ethnic and socioeconomic backgrounds. The loss of the individual is the gain of the group. Individual achievements are discouraged, downplayed and finally eradicated while the group's achievements are encouraged, celebrated and memorialized.

To maintain the unity and cohesion of the cult, there is a clear separation between those "inside" and "outside." Members are holy, special, chosen; outsiders are unholy, ignorant, toxic. Contact with the outside world—often including family—is discouraged, and family is redefined as the group itself. In this new family, subjugation and subservience is expected and obedience and control is demanded. From one's sexuality to one's personal hygiene, the leader possesses unquestioned, absolute authority over its members' lives. For a cult leader, it is imperative to seem infallible, to possess the answers, the solutions, the only route to salvation. The leader is fierce in singular righteousness, in the design to hail oneself absolute. A narcissist with insatiable needs for power, control and, very often, fame, the leader seeks affirmation of supreme authority through alignment with public figures and celebrities, achieving large numbers of recruits and amassing private fiefdoms.

Through the need to please the leader, to ascend the ranks, to work to fulfill the leader's vision, cults dictate followers' actions and thoughts. Obedient members receive exalted status, and conformity is enforced through notions of guilt, shame and failure by both the leader and other members. A system of reporting on members for transgressions creates both an internal police force and opportunities for promotion and rewards for turning in brother and sister members. Those who violate the rules are punished and eventually, to maintain the coherent group unity, expelled. After time, the group assumes all roles—family, friends, church, home, work, community, and departing, whether voluntarily or involuntarily, after years or even decades, without having a concrete safety net is challenging, and sometimes utterly impossible. The world on the other side appears frightening and overwhelming.

Just who is so easily swept up in the group-think and loss of individuality that are hallmarks of cults? A misconception is that there is a certain "type"—usually imbalanced, weak— that not only finds themselves caught inside a cult but that isn't able to extract themselves from it. The truth is, there isn't one typical profile, "type." People with advanced degrees and people without any formal education are both equally likely to find themselves swaddled in orange robes or holed up in a compound. The urge to be a part of something is elemental, raw and natural. To have a defined goal, a purpose, offers meaning. Most people strive for acceptance within social groups and long for affirmation from others. Be it in an office or country club, adjustments are made to conform, to gain approval and to advance.

The Tragedy of Cults

The tragedy of cults is *not* that they victimize the weak-minded or the unintelligent, but that they rob us of the most productive years of some of the people who have the highest potential for making genuinely valuable contributions to the good of our society. The tragedy of cults is that thousands of people have been deceived into giving up their education, hopes and ambitions to follow a rainbow. Some of them have died, some of them have survived.

Mary Kochan, "Cults: The Threat Is Real," Lay Witness, 2003.

Extremism Is the Norm

In cults, extremism is the norm. When hyper-devotion is expected behavior, for acceptance new recruits tend to rapidly thrust themselves into the prescribed lifestyle much to the chagrin of their family and friends on the "outside." There is no blame, no fault for having the audacity to plunge into belief, into faith so deeply, so forcefully that critical and analytical red flags, even if they once appeared, are snapped off. Belief and faith are such intoxicants that logical reason and facts become blurry and nonsensical.

While the boundary between cults and religion often feels confusing—the *Oxford English Dictionary*'s definitions differ only slightly with cults being "small" in size and possessing "beliefs or practices regarded by others as strange or sinister." Deciding what is strange or sinister certainly depends on the beholder. When accusations of being in a cult appear, members quickly and vehemently deny they are in a cult—they are part of a "spiritual path," a "special church," a "progressive movement"—other groups are cults, but not theirs. No way.

Perhaps it is more useful to discern what a religious movement is or what a cult is by comparing its impact upon members' lives: does it complement or control? At their best, healthy religions and organizations complement rich, full lives by offering balance, community, comfort. At their worst, they lapse into vehicles demanding control. Cults limit lives into narrow, claustrophobic existences whose singular purpose is the cult itself.

Cult leaders, experts in psychological manipulation, prey on both the follower's ability to believe and need to belong. But this type of behavior is hardly limited to cults. After all, the aptitude and capacity to exploit human beings is universal, and, with the right ambitious and charismatic leader, any group easily could morph into a cult. What prevents that from occurring is that most established religions and groups have accountability mechanisms that restrain that from happening; cults, however, are purposefully designed so that the only restraints are the ones placed upon the people who, without even realizing it, have just done what they never thought they would do—join a cult.

> *"Though there are occasional exceptions, 'cult' has become little more than a convenient, if largely inaccurate and always pejorative, shorthand for a religious group that must be presented as odd or dangerous."*

The Term Cult Is Misused for New Religious Movements

Douglas E. Cowan and David G. Bromley

Douglas E. Cowan teaches religious studies and the sociology of religion at Renison University College, an affiliate of the University of Waterloo, Ontario, Canada. David G. Bromley is a sociology professor at Virginia Commonwealth University and the University of Virginia. In the following viewpoint excerpted from their book, Cults and New Religions: A Brief History, *Cowan and Bromley claim that the identification of new religious movements (NRMs) as cults is erroneous and derogatory in most cases. Anti-cultists are suspicious of these groups, which often resemble conventional faith groups, because they diverge from common understandings of Christianity, the authors maintain. Furthermore, assumptions that NRMs use brainwashing and*

Douglas E. Cowan, and David G. Bromley, *Cults and New Religions: A Brief History*, Oxford: Blackwell Publishing, 2008. Reproduced by permission of Blackwell Publishers.

prey on mental weaknesses to attract members are not only problematic, argue Cowan and Bromley, but also inhibit insight into this spiritual phenomenon.

As you read, consider the following questions:

1. What do cults epitomize to some and represent to others, as stated in the viewpoint?

2. Why do people have little direct knowledge of cults, in the authors' view?

3. According to the authors, what effectively occurs when a group identifies as a cult?

It should be clear . . . that the debate over what constitutes a "cult" or "new religious movement" is often highly contested and emotionally charged. For some, these new religions epitomize all that is dangerous and deviant in the compass of religious belief and practice. For others, they represent fascinating glimpses into the way human beings construct religious meaning and organize their lives to give shape to religious experience. These differences in understanding, however, are only exacerbated by the different agendas that motivate various interest groups.

On the one hand, some groups proactively challenge the legitimacy of new religious movements, and seek to convince adherents to abandon their new religious commitments. . . . Evangelical counter-cult apologists like Bob Larson consider new religions suspect simply because they either deviate or are altogether different from their own understanding of Christianity. Indeed, new religions are often treated with skepticism when their principal beliefs differ from those of the dominant religious tradition in a particular society. As historian of religions J. Gordon Melton points out, though, this dynamic varies considerably from country to country. "For example," he writes, "in the United States the United Methodist Church is one of the dominant religious bodies. In Greece, the government cited it as being a destructive cult." Thus, what appears as a cult in one context may be one of the most prevalent religious traditions in another. Secular anticult activism, on the other hand, is motivated not by theological conflict or differences in doctrinal belief, but by civil libertarian concerns for the psychological welfare of new religious adherents. . . . For both of these countermovements, however, the same set of salient issues are involved: How do we show that cults are dangerous? How do we warn people against them? And, most importantly, how do we get people to leave them behind?

Little Direct Knowledge

Most people, however, have little direct knowledge of new religious movements. While a relative few may know someone who has joined a group colloquially regarded as a "cult," in reality most people get the majority of their information about new or controversial religions through the media. And, though there are occasional exceptions, "cult" has become little more than a convenient, if largely inaccurate and always pejorative, shorthand for a religious group that must be presented as odd or dangerous for the purposes of an emerging news story. Indeed, news media tend to pay attention to new religions only when something drastic has taken place—the mass suicide of Peoples Temple in Guyana in 1978; the BATF [Bureau of Alcohol, Tobacco, Firearms and Explosives]/FBI [Federal Bureau of Investigation] siege of the Branch Davidian residence in 1993; the 1995 and 1997 murder/suicides in Switzerland and Canada of members of the Order of the Solar Temple; the 1997 suicides of the Heaven's Gate "Away Team"; other preparations for the end-of-the-world-as-we-know-it by groups such as the Church Universal and Triumphant; raids by a variety of official agencies on groups such as the Twelve Tribes and the Children of God/The Family [currently known as Family International]; or the 2000 murder/suicides of the Movement for the Restoration of the Ten Commandments of

God in rural Uganda. Since media representation of virtually any topic is governed first by the principle of negativity—which, in popular terms, means "if it bleeds, it leads"—the only information people generally have of new religious movements occurs in the context of what James Beckford has called the "threatening, strange, exploitative, oppressive and provocative." Because of this, though the vast majority of new religious movements never cross the threshold of a "dramatic dénouement," many are caught up in this kind of negative characterization.

Theological Hubris

Each of these definitions, however, presents its own set of problems. Arguing, as members of the evangelical counter-cult often do, that any religious group other than their own is by definition a cult demonstrates little more than the theological hubris by which many exclusive religious traditions are marked. Indeed, even in the United States, a number of well-known fundamentalist Christian groups could easily be caught up in the net cast by the evangelical counter-cult's definition. Relying on a variety of "thought control" or "brainwashing" metaphors to explain why people join new religions, the secular anticult often contends that cults display a stereotypical set of negative organizational characteristics and practices. The International Cultic Studies Association—which was formerly known as the American Family Foundation, one of the largest of the secular anticult groups that emerged in the 1970s—now lists 15 characteristics it believes are often found in suspect groups. Among other things, these "cultic groups" have a "polarized us-versus-them mentality"; they use "mind-altering practices (such as meditation, chanting, speaking in tongues, denunciation sessions, and debilitating work routines) to excess"; they are "preoccupied with making money" and "with bringing in new members"; and active "members are expected to devote inordinate amounts of time to the group and group-related activities." Scholars have challenged the usefulness of this kind of definitional checklist on three principal grounds: (a) there is no indication how many of these "characteristics" have to be present in order for a group to be considered "cultic"; (b) it does not adequately define what constitutes "excessive" or "inordinate" devotion, practice, or behavior, nor does it demonstrate that these are by definition harmful; and (c) it does not satisfactorily discriminate between those very few religious groups which may actually be dangerous and the vast panoply of other religious and social groups that display similar characteristics but pose little or no threat either to their members or to society at large. Finally, given that new religious movements are almost always presented in the media through the lens of controversy, two major problems emerge. First, with little or no countervailing information readily available, media reporting comes to represent the cultural stock of knowledge about those particular groups. However biased and inaccurate, those reports become the foundation for "common knowledge about cults." Second, because a significant part of "what makes an event news is its ability to galvanize public attention quickly and unambiguously," the negative portrayals of one new religious movement are often quickly, easily, and once again inaccurately generalized to describe all new religions. What the media represents as the case with one group is very often presented as the case for all.

A Fundamental Weakness

Conversely, scholars of new religious movements have long countered that many of the groups that are labeled "cults" often closely resemble a variety of conventional organizations in which these same characteristics are accepted as legitimate or necessary: communes and intentional communities, convents, monasteries, and other high-commitment religious societies, multilevel marketing organizations, and armed forces training and combat units, to name just a few. This confusion has led

An Opportunity Rather than a Menace

New religions certainly address themselves to the eternal question of religious truth; they invoke our emotional and intellectual response; they stimulate us to self-reflection and self-critique; they often foment conflict between individuals and their families and society at large; and they leave many people confused and hurt in their wake. They are, however, more of a challenge than a threat. They present an opportunity rather than a menace. A better way of understanding them and coping with the difficulties they have created or brought into focus is to look on them as both partners and rivals in the religious quest. To panic and react by engaging in verbal or physical attacks, lengthy legal suits, religious crusades, or social reprisals to eradicate them or curtail their activities may lead to more serious problems.

John A. Saliba,
Understanding New Religious Movements.
Walnut Creek, CA: AltaMira Press, 2003.

members of the secular anticult movement to qualify its usage rather dramatically. Margaret Singer, for example, one of the principal intellectuals behind the secular anticult, once wrote: "I have had to point out why the United States Marine Corps is not a cult so many times that I carry a list to lectures and court appearances." If this is the case, then we contend that it is not so much a problem with the audiences to which Singer spoke, but a fundamental weakness in the anticult definition she employed.

Unlike the evangelical counter-cult, the secular anticult, or the mainstream media, most social scientists and religious studies scholars are interested in understanding new religions in their social, cultural, and historical contexts. Where do they come from? Why do they emerge at particular times and in specific places? How do they develop, and what contributes to their evolution, success, and, not infrequently, their decline? Rather than convince adherents to change their allegiances, these scholars want to understand the processes of recruitment and defection, of affiliation and disaffiliation. Why do people join and why do they leave? Are new religious movements, in fact, as dangerous as they are often portrayed in the mass media?

Alternatives to the Term "Cult"

Over the past few decades, social scientists have tried in a variety of ways to rehabilitate the term "cult" for analytic purposes, though these attempts have met with only limited success and in common usage the word still carries unrelentingly negative connotations. Failing that, a number of alternatives have been suggested. While "new religions" or "new religious movements" (NRMs) have become the most common, others include "alternative religious movements," "emergent religions," "controversial new religions," and "marginal (or peripheral) religious movements." None of these is ideal, either. When has a group been around long enough to stop being considered "new"? To what is it "alternative"? What about groups that are both new and alternative, but relatively uncontroversial? And what does it mean to be "marginal"—is that merely a function of group size, or does it involve a more distinctive social stigma? While "emergent religions" seems to address some of these issues, many new religions pass largely unnoticed in society, and this begs the question whether they can be said to have really "emerged" at all. There is no perfect answer.

All these differences and questions notwithstanding, though, one thing is very important to remember . . . : Members of the groups we discuss ... never consider themselves part of a "cult." A few new religions, such as the Raëlians, will admit to being a "cult," but in doing so they have actively redefined the term to strip it of its negative connotations. While adherents of some groups are content to be regarded as members of a new religion, others, such as practitioners of Transcendental Meditation, contend that theirs is not a religious movement at all. Members of the Church of Scientology, on the other hand, insist that theirs is a bona fide religion, despite widespread media and countermovement criticism that it is not. And still others, such as Unificationists, Branch Davidians, or members of the Children of God/The Family, are clear that their faith is not new at all, that they are in fact devout Christians and full members of the largest single religious group on the planet. . . .

We take the position that members of new religions want (and ought) to be taken as seriously as any other religious believer. Any preconceived notions that new religious adherents are brainwashed, spiritually deceived, or mentally ill are not only problematic from an empirical standpoint, but ultimately erect significant barriers to understanding these fascinating social movements more fully. This is why we believe that understanding new religions as sincere (if occasionally problematic) attempts to come to terms with what adherents regard as the most important issues in life is a far more productive endeavor than simply dismissing them as theological imposters, attacking them as social deviants, or capitalizing on them only when they appear newsworthy.

"To analyze the extreme or grotesque forms of cult religion . . . is a way of being more vigilant to false religion in us all."

Cults and Religions Have Important Differences

H. Stephen Shoemaker

In the following viewpoint, H. Stephen Shoemaker contends that specific characteristics separate religious cults from established religions. Unlike legitimate Christian groups, cults have leaders who are godlike figures, break from reality without external references to judge truth, and operate in secrecy, Shoemaker explains. Furthermore, he maintains, cults do not view the world as God's benevolent creation, and they subject members to abuse and authoritarian rule. Shoemaker adds that scripture and apocalyptic literature are falsely interpreted by cults who contradict biblical teachings about the end of time. The author is the senior minister at Myers Park Baptist Church in Charlotte, North Carolina.

As you read, consider the following questions:

1. In the author's view, why is "cult" a slippery term?

H. Stephen Shoemaker, "Ten Marks of a Religious Cult," staging.nambtest.net, Reproduced by permission of the author.

2. What does Shoemaker mean in stating that cults see only life in the cult as good?

3. Compared to Christians, how do cults perceive the world, as stated by the author?

The horror of the [David] Koresh cult tragedy [in which nearly one hundred people died during a 1993 siege near Waco, Texas], (or the destruction of the World Trade [Center] towers in New York by Islamic cultists, ed.) gives us opportunity to ponder the differences between true and false religion; between healthy and unhealthy spirituality. There is some admixture of good and bad religion in all of us. The differences are matters of degree along a continuum. To analyze the extreme or grotesque forms of cult religion like that of Koresh's Branch Davidian community is a way of being more vigilant to false religion in us all.

What we confront in this situation is what we could call "the mystery of evil." There is an inexplicable "more" that turns simple sin into an evil of tragic dimension. We also encounter here the religious expression of a massively unhealthy personality. David Koresh was mentally ill. We can only wish he had received some help along the way.

We could say, unhealthy religion is the kind of religion unhealthy persons have. But we should also say that we are all vulnerable to false religion and unhealthy spirituality, some more than others.

So here are ten marks of false or "cult" religion. The word "cult" is a slippery term. It is used to label any religious group you think is wrong. Early Christians were thought of as a cult by the majority culture. One person's saint is another person's religious fanatic. So we should move carefully. That is why I think it is important to try to describe specific characteristics.

A Godlike Leader

1. The leader assumes godlike authority over its members. In the book of Acts [referring to the Acts of the Apostles, the

fifth book in the New Testament], the townspeople at Lystra think Paul and Barnabas are the Greek gods Zeus and Hermes, and they begin to worship them. Paul and Barnabas show their integrity by being horrified at this worship. They tear their clothes and say, "Stop, we are humans like you" (Acts 14). Leaders like David Koresh enjoy and encourage the worship. They assume perfect knowledge and goodness. They become like a god.

Contrast this with the words of Jesus. When someone addressed him as "good teacher," Jesus responded, "Why do you call me good? No one is good but God alone" (Mark 10:18). The apostle Paul said of his leadership style as opposed to "super apostles" of his day: "Not that we lord it over you in faith; we work with you for your joy" (2 Corinthians 1:24). And Peter gave this instruction: "Tend the flock of God that is in your charge not for shameful gain but eagerly, not as domineering over them . . . but being examples . . ."(1 Peter 5:2–3).

An Escape from Reality

2. It provides an escape from reality. Reality has to do with the truth of things, truth which can be validated by other people. Cult religion provides few "reality checks." A reality check is when you go to another person or to a group and say, "I'm not sure I'm perceiving things correctly. Would you test my perceptions with me?" Cult religion is characterized by distorted thinking and false perceptions. Their doctrinal convictions or views of reality have no checks and balances. There are no external reference points by which to judge the truth of its claims. [Christian theologian] John Wesley provided his followers with a fourfold criterion for the truth of doctrine: scripture, reason, tradition, and experience. Cults have only one reference point: the powerful subjective interpretations of its leader.

[Poet] T.S. Eliot said, "Humankind cannot bear very much reality." Good religion helps us bear a bit more so we might live more healthily. False religion helps us to flee reality. It traffics in magical thinking. Magical thinking imagines magical solutions to problems not based in reality. It says, "If I do or say this, I can get God to act in this way or the world to respond in this way."

Trafficking in Guilt and Shame

3. Cult religion traffics in guilt and shame. It preys upon people with heavy guilt and shame and offers a false solution: total commitment to the cult. Guilt and shame, when healthy, move us to life-changing behavior which leads us to a happier and healthier life. But they can be manipulated to promote unhealthy allegiance to a leader or group.

Presenting Cult Life as Good

4. Cult religion demands a complete break from life to this point. All the "past" is bad or evil. Only present life in the cult is good. God and God's Spirit are not to be located "back there" in earlier experiences of life. Because of this message, it offers a special allure to people who have suffered a painful or abusive past life. But it is false hope, as they will find out.

Thriving in Secrecy

5. Cult religion thrives in secrecy. It creates a secret garden of perfect religion. It hides its doctrines, its rules, its community behavior under the cloak of secrecy. There is a closed circle of membership. Its doctrines are an "esoteric" body of truths which only insiders can know and appreciate.

Breaking Moral Laws from "Above"

6. It breaks moral laws from "above." Sometimes people break moral and societal laws from below—they aren't "good" enough. Others break laws because they think they are too good for them. They think themselves creatures who live above

the laws which "ordinary" people need to observe. [Russian novelist Fyodor] Dostoevsky paints the portrait of such characters in *Crime and Punishment* and *The Brothers Karamazov*: brilliant elitists who think common laws do not pertain to them. Cult religion often thinks its hold on perfect truth excuses them from common ethical, moral, and legal structures of life.

Breaking with the "World"

7. It promotes a complete break with the "world." The Bible speaks of "the world" in two different ways; these balance each other. One use of the word refers to the good creation of God: "The earth is the Lord's and the fullness thereof" (Psalm 24:1). The other refers to the systems and ways of the world which are organized against the way of God: The epistle of John calls us to be "in the world but not of it"(1 John 2).

Cult religion does not see the world as the good creation of God. The world is under the spell of the devil. It is unalterably corrupt. The world will always be against the true and righteous cult. Such a view aids and abets paranoid thinking. The cult sees itself as children of light living in the midst of children of darkness (everybody else).

The famous Yale church historian Jaroslav Pelikan noted that heresy always takes one of two paths. One is the heresy of too much continuity with the world. Its followers identify too much with the ways of the world. This is the liberal tendency; taken too far it becomes heresy. The other way is the heresy of too much discontinuity with the world. The world is corrupt. Redemption has to do with another realm. This is the tendency of fundamentalist thinking; taken too far it becomes heresy.

Cult religion often errs in the second direction. It cuts itself off from the world as the good creation of God. Legal, medical, and social authority is questioned. Reason, science, and the commonsense shared realities of most folk are mistrusted.

Doctrinal Changes and Spiritualistic Practices

A characteristic which has plagued many a cult group is that of *doctrinal changes*. Numerous groups have found shifts in theology to take place after the death of one leader and the replacement by the successor or have made alterations because of inner strife or outside social pressure.

Ties to *spiritualistic practices* is another trait that may be found in several cults. Such activity includes clairvoyance, automatic writings, claimed angelic direction and alleged help in spiritual matters from departed loved ones.

Personal Freedom Outreach,
"Patterns in the Cults," 1986.

Abusing People

8. It is abusive in its way of treating people. Authoritarian rule is imposed. The leaders have perfect truth and goodness and they "lord it over" the rest. They use coercive power, fear, intimidation, and manipulation to keep people in line. If one disagrees with leadership, s/he is of the devil.

Abused people often seek refuge in cults only to reenact their earlier abuse. Personal boundaries are violated by the leader and other members of the community. Healthy boundaries are not honored.

The apostle Paul spoke of the way the Corinthians had been abused by the super apostles who had taken over: "For you bear it if a man makes slaves of you, or preys upon you, or takes advantage of you, or puts on airs, or strikes you in the face" (2 Corinthians 11:20–21).

Dividing the World into Good and Bad

9. Everything is black and white. There is no gray. There is little sense of personal humility or of the Mystery of God. There is no reverent "not-knowing" about God and truth. Everything is perfectly known. The world is divided into the absolute good and bad, the children of God and the children of the devil. Its psychological mechanism is to blame everything on people outside them. It projects its own evil, sin and darkness onto others. [Psychiatrist M.] Scott Peck in his book *People of the Lie* says the root of human evil is denying any darkness or sin inside us and projecting it onto those around us.

Using Scripture to Defend Subjective Truths

10. It uses scripture to defend its subjective version of the truth and to condemn all others. Cult religion especially likes the apocalyptic books of Revelation and Daniel. Apocalyptic literature is highly charged poetic religious literature written in very bad times. For example, Revelation was written during the first empire-wide persecution of Christians by the Roman state. Apocalyptic means literally "unveiling" and apocalyptic literature unveils (or reveals) the truth about what is going on now and the truth about how everything will end up at the end of time. Its basic message is that life is a fight to the finish between the forces of good and evil but that with God's help the forces of good will prevail. Some of the bizarre imagery is code language to refer to what was going on at the time the book was written. For example the "beast" in Revelation 13 refers to Rome. Historical circumstances are illustrative of a larger spiritual battle between God and Satan. And there is a vision of final blessedness when the kingdom of this world will give way to the kingdom of God and eternal blessedness.

False interpretation of the book by cult religion ignores the first-century context and jumps to the present. The cult leader presumes to know the secrets of the book which no one else has ever known. (For example, David Koresh's belief was that he alone knew the meaning of the seven seals.)

Because apocalyptic literature points to the final culmination of things, cult interpretation of the book often uses its new knowledge to prove that now is the final end of things. A person deluded into thinking s/he is the new incarnation of the Messiah may link his or her death with the final battle and end of all things. This may well be what David Koresh thought: his martyrdom would set into motion the end of the world.

In light of this, hear the words of Jesus of Nazareth about the final things when the end is to come: "But of that day or that hour no one knows, not even the angels in heaven, NOR THE SON, but only the Father" (Mark 13:32).

Cult leaders like David Koresh presume to know more than Jesus claimed to know. When someone claims to know more than Jesus, that's a bad sign.

There is mixture of good and bad, true and false, healthy and unhealthy religion in all of us. Powerful unhealthy personalities have the capacity to victimize people when they use religion to prop up their cause and justify their claims. As [French philosopher Blaise] Pascal said hundreds of years ago: "Men never do evil so completely and cheerfully as when they do it from religious conviction."

So let us be vigilant to the false, the bad, the unhealthy in us and in those who would lead us.

"Cult and religion are labels that swing
like a saloon door, and the trick is to
know on which side any of us stands."

Cults and Religions Have Similarities

Brad Hirschfield

Brad Hirschfield is a rabbi and president of the National Jewish
Center for Learning and Leadership. In the following viewpoint,
Hirschfield questions common distinctions between cults and religions. Age and tradition cannot separate the two, as all religions have a clear origin and begin with innovation, he states.
Furthermore, the distinction cannot be based on popular acceptance, Hirschfield states, as cultlike practices are widespread and
many religious groups are obscure. In fact, the author proposes
that all religions, at one point in time, have shown the characteristics of cults.

As you read, consider the following questions:

1. To what does the author compare the case of Ria
   Ramkissoon?

2. What examples does the author provide to support his
   position that age cannot distinguish cults from religions?

Brad Hirschfield, "The Thin Line Between Religions and Cults," *Washington Post*, April
1, 2009. Reproduced by permission of the author.

3. What are the five characteristics of a cult that all religions have exhibited, as described by Hirschfield?

A Baltimore mother accused of joining a cult and starving her child says she was acting on her religious beliefs. What's the difference between extreme religious conviction and delusion? Between a religion and a cult?

In exchange for her cooperation, Maryland prosecutors have offered Ria Ramkissoon a reduced charge in the case against Queen Antoinette who leads a West Baltimore cult known as One Mind Ministries. Ria, and other members of the group, starved Ria's son to death because he did not say "Amen" when he was directed to do so. It's troubling, but probably no worse than similar deals made in courtrooms across the nation every day.

What's really troubling, at least initially, is the story of a woman willing to sacrifice her son because her faith demanded it. But is Ria Ramkissoon's story any worse than the story of a man who waits his whole life to have a child, and then, when he finally does, he carries that child to a mountaintop where he prepares him as an offering to the god who tells him to do so? Is her story worse than that of another father who sends his only son into the world just so he can watch him suffer and die an agonizing death?

There "must" be a difference though, because Ria is a member of a cult and the other stories are those of Abraham's binding of Isaac in the Hebrew Bible, and Jesus' sojourn on Earth as recorded in the New Testament. And those are the founding stories not of cults, but of religions, right? Well, let's see.

The Line Between Religions and Cults

While the passage of time is probably the only way to distinguish between extreme religious conviction and delusion, the same modest claim need not be made for the distinction between a religion and a cult. That line can be demarcated with relative ease, but not in the ways that it usually is.

It's not a function of the too often proffered liberal twaddle that cults are mean and harsh, while real religion is gentle and sweet. It's not, as theological conservatives are want to argue, that their faith is true because "God really said what we believe but not that other stuff." And it's not about it all being the same as the rabid secularists love to claim.

The distinction between cults and religions cannot be based on age, with the new kids on the block labeled cults and the old ones religions. After all every religion has a starting point and each tradition was once considered an innovation. For example, when early Jews proclaimed their faith in one God, and later on early Christians claimed that Jesus was that god's only begotten son, their contemporaries considered each group to be lunatic cultists.

Nor can the distinction between cult and religion be a matter of popular acceptance. Both history and the contemporary world are filled with cultlike practices that are adopted by millions. And many small groups pursue spiritual fulfillment in ways that are not likely to ever gain mass acceptance. So where is the bright line which marks the divide between cults and religions?

The Five Characteristics of Cults

Cults are typically defined by five characteristics. First, cults tend to centralize power in the hands of a single individual or small group that is considered beyond questions. Second, they treat all questions about the group and its beliefs as intolerable challenges to the group's authority and authenticity. Third, they demean all those who do not share their beliefs and sow fear and mistrust amongst their believers about all such people. Fourth, they typically cut off all or most opportunities for members to interact freely with those outside the

Paying Attention to the Fringe

In the beginning, all religions are obscure, tiny, deviant cult movements. Caught at the right moment, Jesus would have been found leading a handful of ragtag followers in a remote corner of the mighty Roman Empire. How laughable it would have seemed to Roman intellectuals that this obscure cult could pose a threat to the great pagan temples. In similar fashion, Western intellectuals scorn contemporary cults. Yet, if major new faiths are aborning, they will not be found by consulting the directory of the National Council of Churches. Rather, they will be found in lists of obscure cult movements. Thus, to assess the future of religion, one must always pay close attention to the fringes of religious economies.

Rodney Stark and William Sims Bainbridge,
The Future of Religion:
Secularization, Revival and Cult Formation.
Berkeley, CA: University of California Press, 1985.

group. And finally, they take revenge upon those who choose to leave the group, in ways which include, cutting them off from all relationships with those who remain inside, confiscation of material goods and even physical harm.

The fact that pretty much every religion has done all of these things at some point in the history of the group means that while the line between cults and religions is clear, it is not fixed or static. In fact, most cults have the capacity to move past the kind of ugly behavior which defines them as a cult. And more importantly, most religions can and do slip into cultlike behavior from time to time. When they remain steadfast in such behavior, however old their tradition, or however popular, they become a cult.

Cult or religion? To paraphrase Forrest Gump's mother, cults are as the cultists do. And the same can be said for religions and their followers. Cult and religion are labels that swing like a saloon door, and the trick is to know on which side any of us stands.

> "What interests me more is the weird
> and sinister belief system of the [Mor-
> mon Church]."

Mormonism and Cults Have Similarities

Christopher Hitchens

In the following viewpoint, Christopher Hitchens contends that Mormonism—whether or not it is a cult—exhibits cultlike characteristics and is based on disturbing and sinister beliefs. The author points out that Mormonism has extreme practices, a supreme leader, and a closed and controlling church that is difficult to leave. Hitchens also accuses the religion of engaging in fraud, racism, and unsettling activities in its past and recent history. Therefore, he believes that Mormons seeking public office should be scrutinized for their beliefs. Hitchens, who died in December 2011, was a noted journalist, literary critic, and author of God Is Not Great: How Religion Poisons Everything.

As you read, consider the following questions:

1. How does the author describe Joseph Smith, founder of the Mormon Church?

2. What example does Hitchens provide to support his allegation that the Mormon Church is racist?

3. What recent activity involving the deceased has the Mormon Church engaged in, as purported by Hitchens?

I have no clear idea whether [Baptist] Pastor Robert Jeffress is correct in referring to the Church of Jesus Christ of Latter-day Saints [LDS], more colloquially known as the Mormons, as "a cult." There do seem to be one or two points of similarity. The Mormons have a supreme leader, known as the prophet or the president, whose word is allegedly supreme. They can be ordered to turn upon and shun any members who show any signs of backsliding. They have distinctive little practices, such as the famous underwear [referring to temple garments worn by adult members of the church], to mark them off from other mortals, and they are said to be highly disciplined and continent when it comes to sex, booze, nicotine, and coffee. Word is that the church can be harder to leave than it was to join. Hefty donations and tithes are apparently appreciated from the membership.

The "Weird and Sinister Belief System" of Mormonism

Whether this makes it a cult, or just another of the born-in-America Christian sects, I am not sure. In any case what interests me more is the weird and sinister belief system of the LDS, discussion of which it is currently hoping to inhibit by crying that criticism of Mormonism amounts to bigotry.

To give some examples, the founder of the church, one Joseph Smith, was a fraud and conjurer well known to the authorities of upstate New York. He claimed to have been shown some gold plates on which a new revelation was inscribed in no known language. He then qualified as the sole translator of this language. (The entire story is related in [biographer and historian] Fawn [M.] Brodie's biography, *No Man Knows My*

History. It seems that we can add, to sausages and laws, churches as a phenomenon that is not pleasant to watch at the manufacturing stage. [Writer] Edmund Wilson wrote that it was powerfully shocking to see Brodie as she exposed a religion that was a whole-cloth fabrication.) On his later forays into the chartless wilderness, there to play the role of Moses to his followers (who were permitted and even encouraged in plural marriage, so as to go forth and mass-produce little Mormons), Smith also announced that he wanted to be known as the Prophet Muhammad of North America, with the fearsome slogan: "Either al-Koran or the Sword." He levied war against his fellow citizens, and against the federal government. One might have thought that this alone would raise some eyebrows down at the local Baptist Church. . . .

Saddling itself with some pro-slavery views at the time of the Civil War, and also with a "bible" of its own that referred to black people as a special but inferior creation, the Mormon Church did not admit black Americans to the priesthood until 1978, which is late enough—in point of the sincerity of the "revelation" they had to undergo—to cast serious doubt on the sincerity of their change of heart.

More recently, and very weirdly, the Mormons have been caught amassing great archives of the dead, and regularly "praying them in" as adherents of the LDS, so as to retrospectively "baptize" everybody as a convert. (Here the relevant book is Alex Shoumatoff's *The Mountain of Names*.) In a hollowed-out mountain in the Mormons' stronghold state of Utah is a colossal database assembled for this purpose. Now I have no objection if Mormons desire to put their own ancestors down for posthumous salvation. But they also got hold of a list of those put to death by the Nazis' Final Solution and fairly recently began making these massacred Jews into honorary LDS members as well. Indeed, when the practice was discovered, the church at first resisted efforts to make them stop.

Whether this was cultish or sectarian it was certainly extremely tactless: a crass attempt at mass identity theft from the deceased.

A Politicized Record

The first time I visited Salt Lake City, in 1970, the John Birch Society bookshop was almost a part of the Tabernacle. Ezra Taft Benson, later to be the president of the church, was a member of its board of 12 Apostles—and sought their approval—when he served in [President Dwight D.] Eisenhower's cabinet for eight years. He was, if not a member of the Birch Society, a strong endorser. His pamphlet, "Civil Rights: Tool of Communist Deception," is well remembered. This was the soil that nurtured [conservative political theorist] Cleon Skousen and the other paranoid elements who in the end incubated [conservative political commentator] Glenn Beck. I merely make the point that the Mormon Church has a distinctly politicized record, and is in a weak position to complain when its leaders are asked political questions that arise directly from their membership.

So far, [2012 Republican presidential hopeful] Mitt Romney, who praised Skousen as recently as 2007, has evaded most questions by acting as if he was being subjected to some kind of religious test for public office. He's been supported in this by some soft-centered types who think that any dislike for any "faith group" is ipso facto proof of some sort of prejudice. Sorry, but this will not wash. I don't think I would want to vote for a Scientologist or a Moonie [a member of the Unification Church founded by Sun Myung Moon] for high office, or indeed any other kind, and I think attempts to silence criticism of such outfits are the real evidence of prejudice. The waters are muddied, of course, by the fact that the first attack on Romney came from a man who is himself a clerical big mouth, exploiting religion for political purposes and handing out [2012 Republican presidential hopeful] Rick Perry endorsements. This is the sort of Southern Baptist who believes, in the words of the old ditty:

> We are the pure and chosen few
> And all the rest are damned
> There's room enough in hell for
> you
> We don't want heaven crammed.

As I pointed out a few weeks ago, Perry has not just accepted Jesus Christ as his personal savior, but has expressed the view that those who do not join him are headed for eternal damnation. He has sought to revise and extend his second set of remarks, but not by much. And he believes in miraculous births from virgins, talking snakes, walking cadavers, and other things that feel distinctly weird and cultish to me. The fact is that what we have here is a clash between two discrepant forms of Christianity, in which the good Pastor Jeffress holds no especially high ground and in which the Latter-day Saints, unless they lie, are among the fastest-growing churches in the United States.

The Mormons apparently believe that Jesus will return in Missouri rather than Armageddon: I wouldn't care to bet on the likelihood of either. In the meanwhile, though, we are fully entitled to ask Mitt Romney about the forces that influenced his political formation and—since he comes from a dynasty of his church, and spent much of his boyhood and manhood first as a missionary and then as a senior lay official—it is safe to assume that the influence is not small. Unless he is to succeed in his dreary plan to borrow from the playbook of his pain-in-the-ass predecessor Michael Dukakis [governor of Massachusetts from 1983–1991], and make this an election about "competence not ideology," he should be asked to defend and explain himself, and his voluntary membership in one of the most egregious groups operating on American soil.

"Actually, there are any number of an-
swers to the question, 'Is Mormonism a
cult?'"

It Does Not Matter if
Mormonism Is a Cult

Michael Riley

In the following viewpoint, Michael Riley challenges the allega-
tion that Mormonism is a cult on the basis of definition. For in-
stance, the author suggests the word "cult" is loaded with nega-
tive connotations and has different meanings, and that some
argue that Mormonism could be considered a "theological" cult,
separate from destructive "sociological" cults. Furthermore, if an
anthropological definition is applied, then religions such as Chris-
tianity and Judaism also began as cults, he maintains. Riley is a
pastor at the Atlantic Highlands First Presbyterian Church in
New Jersey and editorial writer and columnist for the Asbury
Park Press.

As you read, consider the following questions:

1. What answers does Riley offer for the question of
   whether Mormonism is a cult?

Michael Riley, "Mormonism: Is It Truly a Cult?," *Asbury Park Press*, October 23, 2011.
Reproduced by permission.

2. Why do evangelicals oppose Mormonism in terms of scripture, as stated by the author?

3. How was Catholicism treated like a cult in the United States, according to Riley?

Back when I was junior cadet in the army of the Lord, as a freshman at a Baptist-affiliated Christian school, there were various attempts to turn me into a sort of spiritual bigot.

Luckily, those attempts didn't take. It has always amazed me that those of us who preach the infinite love and mercy of God can be so intolerant of those who do not hew to our particular theology.

But religious bigotry runs deep in this country, as Republican presidential candidate Mitt Romney surely knows by now.

If he somehow forgot that fact, or thought that such a thing was behind us as a nation, he was reminded a couple of weeks ago, when Dallas pastor Robert Jeffress, a [Republican presidential hopeful] Rick Perry supporter, declared that Christians shouldn't vote for Romney because, as a member of the Church of Jesus Christ of Latter-day Saints, he belongs to a "cult."

Actually, there are any number of answers to the question, "Is Mormonism a cult?"

Among them:

"It depends on what you mean by cult."

"One man's cult is another man's deeply held faith."

"Of course it's not a cult. The next thing you know, this preacher is going to say nasty things about Donny and Marie Osmond."

"Sure, Mormonism is a cult. So what? This is America."

Mormons in Good Company

Back in 1976, as a religion major at Eastern College in Pennsylvania, there was no question that Mormons were a cult. We even had student assemblies to make sure we all knew it. But according to the college, the Church of Jesus Christ of Latter-day Saints was just the tip of the heterodox iceberg. Mormons were part of a cult, sure, but so were the Jehovah's Witnesses and the Seventh-day Adventists. And frankly, many in the student body weren't sure about Roman Catholics, either, what with their incense and purgatory, and their popes and their saints.

It all seems so silly now.

But from the point of view of conservative evangelicals, it's easy to see why Mormons raise ire and eyebrows.

First, they regard Mormonism as a Johnny-come-lately addition to the world religion stage. Coming out of a spiritual revival in the early 19th century called the Second Great Awakening, the Church of Jesus Christ of Latter-day Saints began with a series of visions and revelations given to one Joseph Smith, in 1820. It involved angels and golden plates, and a new testament proclaiming, among other things, that after Easter, Jesus preached to the North American Indians, which came as quite a shock to those who searched their Bibles in vain for any post-resurrection North American visit by Jesus.

Second, the Mormon understanding of such doctrines as the nature of God and the route to heaven are at odds with orthodox Christian teachings. For example, Smith taught that God started out as a human being, and that heaven has different levels, sort of like decks on a cruise ship. And one of the founding doctrines of Mormonism was its belief that all other churches had become corrupt and apostate.

Scripture Alone Not Enough

Another issue that especially rankles evangelicals is that the Mormons do not hold to the doctrine known as "sola scriptura"—scripture alone—which says that the Bible is all a Christian needs to learn about Jesus. For Mormons, the Bible alone is not enough to tell everyone everything they need to

Cartoon by Pat Bagley and CagleCartoons.com.

know about God and life. Apparently, God had a few more details to clear up for humanity. Hence, the Book of Mormon was delivered via Smith to the world.

But "cult" is a word with a lot of baggage. Many people think of a cult as a group that brainwashes folks into believing and behaving in nontraditional ways. But cults come in all sizes and shapes.

Jeffress himself has tried, inelegantly, to distinguish the kind of cult he considers Mormonism—a "theological" cult— from what he calls "sociological" cults. Presumably, "sociological" cults are the sort of murder/suicide/cult Jim Jones was running in Guyana back in the 1970s, or Sun Myung Moon's Unification Church mass weddings, or those folks who offed themselves while wearing sneakers and waiting for the mother ship to whisk them away.

You have to wonder what Pastor Jeffress would think about Thomas Jefferson if he ran for president today. In 1819, Jefferson made up his own Bible, cutting and pasting verses together from the gospels and eliminating all the miracles, angels and any mention of Christ's divinity. That's some serious editing, and would have caused a real brouhaha in any candidate debate.

More than a few of the Founders, including Jefferson, were not Jeffress-style Christians so much as they were Deists, those who believed in an impersonal God who set the universe in motion but didn't take an active role in the life of humanity. And a couple of the "Who's Who" of the American Revolution were outright atheists—Thomas Paine, to name one.

Clearly, their decidedly unorthodox theology did not stop America from getting off to a rousing start.

America has always been a hotbed of dissension over theological purity. The anti-Catholic strain of prejudice goes back to the beginning of the colonies. Colonial charters and laws contained specific proscriptions against Roman Catholics having any political power.

In fact, it was the hatred of Catholics that united many disparate Protestants. That hatred reached its peak in the 19th century when it was tied up with xenophobia and anti-immigrant politics. All those Irish and German settlers were too much for the majority of Americans.

And those attitudes never really went away. In 1960, John F. Kennedy had to answer the worries of voters who thought that if he were elected, he'd be taking his orders from the pope. Well, that was a half century ago. We're beyond that now, you might think.

Another Christian GOP [Grand Old Party or Republican] presidential contender, Rep. Michele Bachmann, belonged for years to the Salem Evangelical Lutheran Church in Stillwater, Minn., which belongs to the Wisconsin Evangelical Lutheran Synod. The synod believes the pope is the Antichrist.

Sometimes, it seems that the only thing that unites these evangelical politicians is their agreement that [President Barack] Obama's longtime pastor, the Rev. Jeremiah Wright, is a radical heretic.

But if we all take a deep, cleansing breath, untwist our knickers and say a quiet prayer, we might be able to take the long view—on a couple of levels. We may see, for example, that often people do not live up to what they say they believe anyway. [Former president] Bill Clinton, anyone? And [former president Richard] Nixon was a Quaker, for God's sake.

Let's also remember that the anthropological definition of culture is a group of people with their own set of religious practices. In that sense, Judaism began as a cult, one of many in the ancient Near East.

And Christianity began as a sect of Judaism—that hardy band of Jewish zealots who had a special relationship with the carpenter's kid who claimed that he rose from the dead. This sect stayed a part of Judaism until the first century, when it left or was kicked out of Judaism and became its own religion.

The Roman Empire soon declared the church a dangerous and seditious cult and set about to destroy it, right up until Emperor Constantine converted to the faith and made the empire Christian.

Finally, at that point, Christians could start declaring heretics left and right, which they did with a vengeance, with inquisitions, witch trials and pogroms.

There is something about believing we have a handle on the truth that leads people to start drawing theological lines in the sand, bloody or otherwise.

Which may be why those semi-heathens who wrote the Constitution put this in Article VI of the document: "no religious Test shall ever be required as a Qualification to any Office or public Trust under the United States."

Purity of faith, or even purity of doctrine, should have no bearing on one's vote.

If you ask me, the only difference Romney's faith might make to most Americans, believers and unbelievers alike, were he to be elected president is that he might have the Mormon Tabernacle Choir sing at his inauguration instead of Aretha Franklin or Bruce Springsteen.

We'll live.

| *"Something dangerous about Scientology is that they truly believe that they are the 'only salvation' for mankind."*

Scientology Is a Dangerous Cult

Amy Scobee, as told to Mike Hess

Amy Scobee is a former member and employee of the Church of Scientology and author of Scientology: Abuse at the Top. *Mike Hess is managing editor of Celebuzz, an entertainment website. In the following viewpoint, Scobee claims that the Church of Scientology betrays its moral code of love and compassion, engaging in wide-scale abuse and civil rights violations. She alleges that members are assaulted to correct behavior, placed into slave labor, forcibly separated from their families, and controlled by withholding information. Additionally, Scientology attempts to silence its critics through threats and defamation, Scobee claims, and uses its status as a religion to conceal its wrongdoings.*

As you read, consider the following questions:

1. According to Scobee, why does Scientology recruit celebrities?

Amy Scobee, interviewed by Mike Hess, "Ex-Scientologist Reveals Details Behind 'Dangerous Cult,' Tom Cruise in New Book," www.Popeater.com, May 13, 2011. © 2012 AOL Inc. Popeater and the Popeater logo are trademarks of AOL Inc. Reproduced by permission.

2. What does Scobee claim she was subjected to during Scientology's purification treatment?

3. What occurs in the organization's Rehabilitation Project Force, as claimed by Scobee?

Most people know very little about Scientology aside from the fact that Tom Cruise, John Travolta and other celebrities are a part of it, and that it's had its fair share of controversy over the years. A new book is looking to pull back the curtain on the mysterious religion founded by L. Ron Hubbard, and the author certainly knows her stuff. Amy Scobee is a former Scientologist who was in the church for more than two decades, and worked in the all-important Celebrity Centre [International] portion of the organization. In her just-released book, *Scientology: Abuse at the Top*, Scobee details all of the troubling things she saw that made her flee what she once called her trusted religion, but now refers to as a "dangerous cult." Scobee spoke exclusively to PopEater over e-mail about her shocking book, her time with Tom Cruise and other Scientology bigwigs, and the (her words) brainwashing, systematic violence and slave labor camps she saw during her 27 years there. . . .

[PopEater:] Could you explain your role within the Church of Scientology?

[Amy Scobee:] I worked in the upper management of Scientology for two decades. For a good portion of that time, I was responsible for the international network of Celebrity Centres, which service people in the field of the arts, government and sports—people with high profiles in the world who are capable of creating a lot of influence on the population.

You were a member for 27 years. What was the spark plug for your departure?

I became less and less tolerant of the abuse that I witnessed as it got more and more harsh. People were very unhappy, family members were being separated, David Miscavige [the current "leader" of Scientology] committed assault and battery on my friends on numerous occasions. I could not justify continuing to support such an organization bent on threats and severe human rights violations, which were a dichotomy of the stated goals and reason I joined in the first place. I wanted to help people and create a better world based on love and compassion for mankind.

Scientology and Celebrities

Why is there such a big push to recruit celebrities to Scientology?

A strategic priority for Scientology is to bring in big-name celebrities as they can influence whole populations. If they endorse Scientology, then masses will want to join, as well. That means expansion, more money, more members who in turn bring in others. The stated goal for Celebrity Centre is to make celebrities into "walking success stories" of Scientology so they promote their success and attribute it to what they learned in Scientology.

In the press, there are often articles that are negative toward the church. Why would they want to attract more celebrities, and in turn, more attention?

They think that any negative press is just a result of "disgruntled ex-members" and should be ignored.

Tom Cruise is by far the most known Scientologist. What types of interaction did you have with him during your time there, and what can you say about him as a person?

I met Tom Cruise and members of his family. I did a project to locate Scientologists for him to hire in order to fill specific positions in his household—such as executive housekeeper, maid, cook, nanny. Personally, I do not have much respect for Tom at all for a few very important reasons. First of all, I think he has abused his "power" as a well-known figure to gain special favors from Scientology. I know of several examples of this, including the fact that I was personally assigned to select his personal entourage, which had nothing to do with my job at the time. I was a full-time staff member in the Sea Organization. I did not get paid for that service; I did not get thanked for that service. I was at the international management base in Hemet [a city in California] when he came to do Scientology services for an extended period of time. The staff members there were not set up to service a celebrity at that property. People were pulled off their own jobs to cater to him. I knew of people [Sea Org members] doing his laundry, supervising him in the course room, supervising his counseling. The music studio conference room was converted to a course room for him; many staff members were utilized to establish audio-visual facilities in his home. Many staff members had to stay up day and night, because on the 500-acre property there were some brown patches on the lawns—it's in the middle of the desert in Hemet. Those brown patches could be seen by helicopter per David Miscavige, and Cruise was going to arrive via helicopter, so we laid sod for days—night and day.

The other factor is that Tom Cruise has proclaimed David Miscavige to be a "LEADER OF LEADERS" and announced to all Scientologists attending the International Association of Scientologists event in 2004 that David Miscavige was the best leader and said that he should know "because I've met them ALL." That's an arrogant statement, plus David Miscavige viciously beats his staff members. So to give Miscavige all this praise puts in concrete to Scientology followers to listen to this "leader" who has NO BUSINESS being in that position because he's DANGEROUS.

Recently, reports surfaced claiming that David Miscavige played Tom Cruise's confession tapes—which are meant to be private—to fellow church members for a laugh over drinks. Does that seem like something he'd do, or have you known this to be true?

Yes—David Miscavige talked about people's private confidential information. I witnessed this myself. I included some specifics of this in my book regarding another celebrity. He also did it to staff—snickering about things that came up in their confessionals and TELLING the specifics to whoever was at the meeting with him at the time. He did that to me. And he did that to many, many others; including calling all-base staff briefings and reporting embarrassing details about supposed transgressions in order to intimidate people. One of my friends told me how Miscavige and he were standing outside when staff were walking between buildings—like for lunch break or something—and he pointed to random people giving "tidbits" on each one as they passed, to "prove" how much "in the know" he is. It's a complete violation of the priest-penitent privilege and a total invasion of privacy.

What was the church's reaction to his showdown with [television host] Matt Lauer?

I was already out of Scientology when that happened. I saw the show and thought Tom was being very arrogant toward Matt Lauer. I don't know what the church response was because I wasn't there, but I presume they would have patted Tom on the back for "standing up" to Lauer and telling the world how bad psychiatric drugs are for people.

Scientology often gets criticized for mobilizing when there's a tragedy (9/11 [the September 11, 2001, terrorist attacks on the United States], the Haiti earthquake [in 2010]) as people feel they're trying to recruit. What can you share on that?

They ARE trying to recruit and create good PR [public relations] for Scientology—"good works, well publicized" is the goal, so as to become more accepted in society and to bring in new members. People are instructed to video [tape] their actions and get media if they can so this can then be shown at their very frequent PR events to "prove" to their members how much they are accepted and expanding and doing good for the world.

Do you think more and more celebrities will lean toward Scientology as time goes on, or has it hit its high point star-wise?

No. Scientology celebrities are already beginning to turn away and have publicly resigned their membership. Award-winning writer/director Paul Haggis, actor Jason Beghe and actor Larry Anderson are a few recent examples. I think more celebrities will walk away as they discover the truth and cease turning a blind eye to the blatant human rights violations so many people are exposing inside Scientology.

Treatment and Tools

During an interview with ABC, you detail your experience with Scientology's purification treatment. You eventually began taking massive amounts of niacin, which led to some side effects. Could you detail that?

The purification program is supposed to be relatively short, where you exercise for a period of time per day and then sweat in the sauna in order to rid the body of any residual drugs and toxins. Miscavige decided that executives in International Management were "incompetent" as they were "dead heads" due to past drug histories being "unhandled." So he decided to create a weird variation of the purification program where many of us were put in the sauna 5 hours per day for MONTHS, at a time. I was on it for 8 months and I know of several others who were on even longer. You take high dosages of niacin—5000 mg [milligrams] per day—while on this program. I got freaked out that my body was being damaged. I had gray matter coming out of my pores and I asked if it could please be checked into by the lab or doctor, which was never done. This is the point when I started to plan my escape from that place. I felt trapped, and at risk both physically and mentally. And it didn't help to have an abusive and nasty leader dictating our lives at that point either. I was sent to Florida and I left from there in March 2005.

What good things are there that Scientology does that people may not know about?

I believe that the study of technology has really helped people because I've read many rave success stories—where people who could not learn before obtained simple tools to be able to read and learn and increase their competence as a result. One doesn't have to be a Scientologist to apply the basic tools of study, such as using a dictionary to clear words and terms one doesn't understand in order to obtain a conceptual understanding of what you are reading and to study a subject on a gradient and to balance the significance with the actual mass of what you're learning—such as LOOK at the piece of equipment while reading the manual!

Scientology believes that one is a spiritual being that has lived before and will continue to live. This is not unique to Scientology, but a basis of a lot of religions. They do promote a moral code of love and compassion and following the laws of the land, which is helpful to those who will actually apply those concepts.

For "the Greater Good"

What are some of the worst things?

Family disconnection and their manipulation, blackmail and control through the threat of being cut off from family, which has devastating effects, and being denied your "only road to salvation as a spiritual being."

The Rehabilitation Project Force [RPF], which I cover in detail in my book. This is a slave labor camp within the Sea Organization where people who have supposedly messed up get sent for sometimes years and years. They are separated from family, segregated from the rest of the group, made to run everywhere, put on hard manual physical work and paid 1/4 the regular staff pay—about $12 per WEEK. I've known several people on that program for over a decade for minor offenses. It's inhumane and that "program" should be shut down.

The way Scientology goes after critics. It's their policy to utterly annihilate the credibility of anyone speaking out against the "church." They have done brutal things in the past along these lines and are still pulling these stunts currently. I've been followed by private investigators—sometimes several at a time, my family's house watched, they've tried to get my in-laws (never even in Scientology) to kick me out of the family, which they refused and dismissed as a completely insane and evil proposal. They put out publications with vicious false and defamatory information about me to hopefully make the readers think I was incapable of accurately reporting on my observations with regards to their illegal activities.

Another key thing is INFORMATION CONTROL. This is a form of mind control. If one controls what you can and cannot see or hear, one is unable to make a rational decision about that matter. Scientology specializes in information control—one is banned from upper levels of "spiritual enlightenment" if it is discovered that you read anything negative about Scientology or talked to someone about it. People are put in for routine confessionals to find out if you "committed this sin." So you are careful to avoid any contact with the media when it comes to Scientology or to read about any exposure about what is going on at the highest echelons. If the general public knew, they would stop supporting Scientology. They would walk away. They'd have the INFORMATION to be able to make that decision. Instead, all they hear is what the head of Scientology (Miscavige) reports at their frequent PR events—how the expansion is better than ever and popularity of Scientology is at an all-time high, etc. They applaud, thinking it's all wonderful and donate a lot of money for the cause to "keep the expansion going." It's very sad. I want people to have the truth. When I informed a family member of mine, who had been a dedicated Scientologist for about 30 years, what was really going on at the top of his church, he chose to walk away and he has officially resigned. That's the logical thing to do. He still believes the technology itself is beneficial, but will no longer support that organization—in fact he has also now requested all of his money back.

Something dangerous about Scientology is that they truly believe that they are the "only salvation" for mankind. They therefore consider they can do all sorts of things—even if it breaks the law—because it's "the greatest good" and forwards their overall mission to ensure everyone's future eternity. Crush a critic into silence, lie on national television, beat a staff member who is not behaving as you'd like, blackmail people using family disconnection and other threats to keep them in line, use personal information obtained on people to smear their name, keep people on the RPF for years, force staff to work around the clock for almost no pay, hide evidence that could be damning if it were discovered—on and on. They are fanatics about being the ONLY salvation and the end justifies the means.

A Destructive Cult

Germany recently declared Scientology a cult. Do you think that's an accurate definition?

Yes—I believe Scientology is actually a dangerous cult. By definition, a "destructive cult" is a religion or other group which has caused or has a high probability of causing harm to its own members or to others. Some researchers define "harm" in this case with a narrow focus, specifically groups which have deliberately physically injured or killed other individuals, while others define the term more broadly and include emotional abuse among the types of harm inflicted. Both physical and spiritual/mental abuse has occurred, and from what I understand is continuing to occur, within Scientology—at its highest ranks. I observed quite a bit of such destructive action and this is detailed in my new book.

Is there a single most-shocking incident or occasion that stands out in your mind from your time in Scientology?

Yes—my realization that I had just spent 27 years of my life supporting what I now realize is a dangerous and destructive cult—a so-called "religion" that hides behind its status as a "church" to cover up crimes and major human rights violations. My own personal integrity is intact and I am determined to expose the abuse to hopefully put it to an end.

| *"The future of Scientology . . . lies in its ability to retain its identity as religion and community . . . while losing the ideological totalism that makes it cultic for many."*

Scientology Is More than Just a Cult

Janet Reitman

In the following viewpoint, Janet Reitman states that Scientology is a religious organization with the potential to become an established religion. Reitman addresses the controversies surrounding Scientology—such as ideological control, regimented discipline, and servitude of its members. Nonetheless, she contends that it serves as a community and religion to many, especially for individuals who grow up as Scientologists. For its identity as a religion, the author says the organization must lose its cultic practices. Reitman is author of Inside Scientology: The Story of America's Most Secretive Religion *and contributing editor at* Rolling Stone.

As you read, consider the following questions:

1. How does the author describe Scientology?

2. What does the author find attractive about Scientology?

3. In what context may Scientology resemble a cult, as stated by the author?

Since 1993, Scientology, which many people have long considered to be a "cult," has been a religion in the eyes of the United States government, with the tax exemption that goes along with that. But whether it is actually a "religion" in the way that most of us think about religion is a wholly different matter.

To address the basics: There is no God in Scientology. There is also no prayer, no concept of Heaven or Hell, no turn-the-other-cheek forgiveness or love, nor any of the other things we typically associate with religion, at least in the Judeo-Christian context. There is also no "faith"—no concept of belief. Instead, there is knowledge, a certainty beyond a shadow of a doubt that Scientology's doctrine, all of which was authored by the church's founder, L. Ron Hubbard, is the absolute *truth*.

A Global Spiritual Enterprise

I like to describe Scientology as a global spiritual enterprise—a religious corporation with a far greater emphasis on the "corporate," profit-making side of the ledger. Since its founding in 1954, Scientology has appealed to people initially as self-help, something Americans, and many others, have been more than willing to pay for. And as self-help, Scientology essentially promises that there are techniques one can learn—through the rigorous study and exact application of L. Ron Hubbard's ideas—that can, for instance, help a person overcome their shyness, or empower them to end a bad marriage, or help them sell themselves more effectively in the workplace. But there is also a spiritual component to Scientology, which has to do with people realizing, through the counseling known as "auditing," that they have lived many past lives. That's where the religion comes in.

When I was reporting on Scientology, I was amazed by the number of ordinary people I met who truly knew—not just believed, but claimed to know—that they had lived before and would live again. That meant death was no longer scary! It also meant that we might even remember our prior lives so saying goodbye to friends and family would *not* really be a "goodbye." Even to me, a person who is agnostic about most religion, it was attractive.

That is what draws people deeply "in" to Scientology. And once in, Scientology becomes different things to different people. One woman I know compares Scientology to an onion. The outer layer, where the celebrities tend to be, is a place where people experience the church as self-help and community. For stars like Tom Cruise or John Travolta, it is the safest of communities because celebrities are catered to in Scientology in both a material way, with added perks and private counseling sessions, but also in a way that shields them from critics or intrusion into their private lives. Wealthy Scientologists are also considered "celebrities" because they tend to donate the most money and involve themselves most in Scientology causes, all of which raises their status.

Much is made of the celebrities in Scientology, though their numbers are very few—there are maybe a dozen actual "celebrities" who belong to the church. But these people serve a promotional function, and because of it are treated like rare birds, put on pedestals by all members, including church staff who endeavor to keep their experience in Scientology positive. This leads to profound isolation from some of Scientology's harsher truths. Celebrities certainly would not be aware of any abuse or harsh treatment of Scientology staff, which, though Scientology officials deny it, has been alleged numerous times by ex-officials over the years. While they would be obliged to obey the policy of "disconnection," by which church members shun anyone, including their closest friends or family members, who leave Scientology on bad terms, they would also tend to believe the word of church officials far more than "apostates," as those who have left Scientology and spoken out are called.

Screenwriter/director Paul Haggis, for instance, believed a senior Scientology official when he pledged that the Church of Scientology did not back the California antigay marriage bill, something the church—along with many other religious organizations—did in fact support. When Haggis discovered the truth, it propelled him to leave the church altogether. But Haggis is, so far, somewhat unique in that he did discover the truth. No Scientologist—be they celebrities or ordinary members—is supposed to read general media reports about the church. These pieces—anything critical—is considered off-limits or "entheta" in the lexicon of the Church of Scientology, and thus harmful to a member's spiritual progress. The truth is what they know via L. Ron Hubbard; media criticisms of Scientology, on the other hand, are to Scientologists, lies or "religious bigotry." Thus they remain very much in the dark; they will not, assuredly, be reading my new book *Inside Scientology: The Story of America's Most Secretive Religion.*

A Significant Challenge

Beyond celebrities, the average middle-class person, who for most of its history has formed the bulk of Scientology's membership, has a far different experience in Scientology. For them, the deeper they are drawn into Scientology, the more indebted to it they become. In some cases, members have been driven into bankruptcy, forcing them to work for the church to continue to afford Scientology counseling. Once they sign up to work for Scientology, their experience turns more punitive: They work extremely long hours, at very low pay, and are expected to adhere to a paramilitary-style discipline that is absent in any workplace I've ever heard of outside of the United States military. At the innermost level of this management, within the Sea Organization, which is the senior management body of the church, there is far more, if not total, ideological control over members, strict adherence to the demands of a leader who has cast himself as a sort of pope, and many other things that would define Scientology, in that context as a more traditional "cult."

But it is only a cult to some. To others it is a community. To others it is self-help. And to others, it is absolutely religion—and in the case of young people who've grown up in the church it is the only religion they've ever known. I think the future of Scientology, if it has one, lies in its ability to retain its identity as religion and community, and even self-help, while losing the ideological totalism that makes it cultic for many. It is a significant challenge, and one that the church in its current incarnation may not be able to shoulder, but it is also the only way, in my opinion, that Scientology will become an enduring, and evolving, religion.

Periodical and Internet Sources Bibliography

The following articles have been selected to supplement the diverse views presented in this chapter.

John Cook	"Cult Friction," *Radar Magazine*, April 2008.
Mark Driscoll	"Is Mormonism a Cult?," Pastor Mark Driscoll, October 18, 2011. http://pastormark.tv.
Darren Ford	"Church of Scientology: Mad, Bad, but Not Nearly as Dangerous as the Big Faiths," *Sabotage Times*, March 22, 2011.
Mitch Horowitz	"When Does a Religion Become a Cult?," *Wall Street Journal*, February 25, 2011.
Patrick Mason, as told to Joanna Brooks	"Why Do Southerners Call Mormonism a Cult?," *Religious Dispatches*, October 10, 2011.
Richard J. Mouw	"My Take: This Evangelical Says Mormonism Isn't a Cult," *Belief Blog*, October 9, 2011. http://religion.blogs.cnn.com.
Mark Oppenheimer	"For the Love of Xenu," *Slate*, July 31, 2007. www.slate.com.
Erik Rush	"Cults of Personalities," Renew America, April 25, 2008. www.renewamerica.com.
Tim Whiston	"The Christian Cult: Brainwash and Mind Control in the Name of the Lord?," ExChristian.net, November 7, 2008. http://articles.exchristian.net.
Richard Zwolinski	"Cult or Religion?," *Therapy Soup*, November 30, 2011. http://blogs.psychcentral.com.

CHAPTER 2

Are Cults a Serious Threat?

Chapter Preface

In 2008 the Russian city of Yaroslavl was shocked by the gruesome murders of three teenage girls and one boy, committed by six satanic teens that lured them into a forest to drink alcohol around a bonfire. On two consecutive days in June—killing two a night—they stabbed each victim 666 times, then dismembered, cooked, and ate some parts of their bodies. After burying the remains in a pit, the group marked it with a dead cat and upside-down crucifix, which was discovered that August. Two years later, the regional court of Yaroslavl found all six members guilty of murder—four guilty of desecrating the bodies. Each member received a prison sentence, the longest of which was set at twenty years for the cult's leader.

Some commentators purport that the threat of satanic cults is real. In early 2009, the Christian Coalition of America warned of the emergence of a new group, the Order of Nine Angles. "This cult encourages and teaches actual human sacrifice, crime, molestation, racism, and extreme liberalism," the coalition states. "I would encourage and urge those of us who are truly concerned for our youth to look further into this cult and educate themselves and their loved ones." On the other hand, critics argue that satanic cults are essentially a myth and the product of moral panic. "There are no satanic cults as organizations, not even as minuscule groups," maintains Jeffrey S. Victor, author of *Satanic Panic: The Creation of a Contemporary Legend*. He suggests that special interest groups use this myth to promote their religious ideologies or for profit, and that murderers identifying as satanists did not belong to an organization or killed in ways that completed a ritual. In the following chapter, the authors assess and deliberate the dangers of cults in contemporary society.

| *"Cults are inherently dangerous. In fact, few things are more dangerous and destructive."*

Cults Are Prone to Crime and Violence

Tom O'Connor

In the following viewpoint, Tom O'Connor asserts that cults have destructive tendencies that are harmful to society and their members. Cult violence, he claims, can be difficult to predict and may be homicidal or suicidal. O'Connor elucidates the warning signs of cults as apocalyptic thinking, a charismatic and dominating leader, paranoia and demonization of outsiders, and stockpiling of weapons and poisons. O'Connor is an associate professor of criminal justice and director of the Institute for Global Security Studies at Austin Peay State University.

As you read, consider the following questions:

1. What does O'Connor suggest are people's views and assumptions of cults?

2. How are cults different from sects, in the author's view?

3. What occurs during the "paranoia warning sign" stage of a cult, as told by O'Connor?

Tom O'Connor, "Cult Crimes," www.drtomoconnor.com, July 14, 2011. Reproduced by permission of the author.

Tragically, all religions justify violence, but so-called "cults" tend to be very harmful to society as well as their own members. Cult violence is a form of collective behavior characterized by progressive escalation of conflict, internal radicalization, and the impossibility of escape or retreat from the inevitability of extreme violence. In short, cults are inherently dangerous. In fact, few things are more dangerous and destructive. Witness the well-known media cases of them, such as the Jonestown massacre, the Branch Davidians, Heaven's Gate, Solar Temple, or Aum Shinrikyo, and one will quickly surmise that they are indeed dangerous, at least as dangerous, if not more so, than terrorism.

Little is known about the causes and dynamics of cult violence. Many people assume that "authorities" have them under surveillance (not true). Infiltration is about the only law enforcement technique that works, and cults are highly sensitive to this. Many people think they aren't a problem as long as they kill their own members (the so-called "somebody else's religion" syndrome). Many people are tolerant of cults because they see them as start-up religions that simply haven't acquired enough real estate yet. Some people are tolerant of cults because they don't see the dangerousness aspect to them. Others avoid talking about them out of political correctness or because they fear getting sued for insulting them. It is time to start paying serious academic attention to cults.

Cults and Sects

There are similarities and differences between sects and cults. Both sects and cults tend to be quite dogmatic with coherent ideologies, and both tend to believe they hold the "one true way" to truth and salvation. However, a sect simply encourages *thought reform* among its members. A cult systematically engages in *mind control*, in a way that jeopardizes the health and safety of its members. For example, a sect encourages its members to go without food (fast) for several days. A cult deliberately [starves] its members (for their own good). Technically, a sect is an offshoot of an established religion. Its leaders tend to come from the lower classes, and they sympathize with the lower classes. In fact, one of the common characteristics of a sect is a disdain for the habits of the wealthy. Cult leaders tend to come from the upper classes, and they hate the lower classes. Sects either die off or expand into established denominations, depending upon how well they embrace or try to play politics. Cults tend to reject politics except for when the ultimate showdown comes with outer-worldliness. Sects get violent progressively while in political manipulation mode (we call this sectarian violence). Cults get violent suddenly and without warning in a kind of rabid, feverish outbreak that someone will undoubtedly say we should have seen coming (we call this lunatic fringe violence).

Cults, to be fair, tend to mostly produce low-level, small-group violence. They can also produce lone-wolf violence. Their pattern is difficult, but not impossible, to predict. They may be most violent when they claim to have invented something completely new and fantastic OR when they claim to have discovered something lost and forgotten. They may come to a sudden demise when their leader dies OR they may re-emerge stronger and more dangerous under a new leader. Leadership succession is critical, but most cults don't prepare for it. The inability to groom successors is the proverbial downfall of all megalomaniacs and narcissists. Some cult leaders have more serious psychological problems; they can also be a sadist. In other cases, they will manipulate their followers and audiences by playing the role of weak, helpless victim. When the cult has a doomsday orientation, it may be unclear whether they have more suicidal than homicidal tendencies, or vice versa. It may very well be when the group is at its most uncertain when they are most dangerous and destructive. However, standard warning signs exist.

Warning Signs

1. apocalyptic thinking, or eschatology, that the world is coming to an end, and true believers will enjoy unique rewards at end-time

2. charismatic leadership where the leader dominates the followers spiritually, emotionally, and sexually

3. paranoia and demonization of outsiders, accompanied by intellectual isolation within a cloistered community

4. preparations of an unusual nature, usually indicated by a buildup of guns, poisons, and/or weapons of mass destruction

Arguably, the most dangerous stage is the paranoia warning sign. This is usually a highly visible stage. Many cults publish some book or treatise by the leader, usually rich in paranoia. When they publish, they transform into what are called "audience cults" and membership may enlarge to those who have read the book, but never met. This is often when "lone wolf" radicalization takes place. The "book" may imply a call for the establishment of leaderless cells or some kind of criminal action, but it will definitely produce a marketable and measurable effect among the membership. A splinter group or spin-off group may also emerge in response to publication of a book. In what is the more usual pattern, an audience cult usually becomes a "client cult," which describes a group of regular customers who seek to purchase more products, goods, books, or services that are associated with the cult. The group becomes mobilized, one individual at a time, and the membership becomes ready for preparations. This is how a cult movement gets momentum besides word of mouth and family indoctrination.

[Baptist minister and historian on religion Charles] Kimball's book, *When Religion Becomes Evil: Five Warning*

Signs, is quite informative. His five warning signs include the following, which are curiously similar to what terrorist groups do:

1. absolute truth claims

2. blind obedience

3. establishing the "ideal" time

4. the end justifies the means

5. declaring holy war

It's often said that something "evil" is something that's disrespectful of other beliefs and all the moral customs and principles of society. By establishing absolute truth claims, a group sets itself up as separate from regular society and lays claim to a "higher moral authority." At this point, they have managed to convert evil into something which looks good. Blind obedience characterizes an authoritarian-like, unquestioning attitude inside the group; rebelliousness and subversion characterize activity outside the group. Discipline is established, almost like a rigid chain of command, with strict rules on how to behave toward insiders and outsiders. Establishing the "ideal" time for total rebellion may or may not be tied to the group's vision of an ideal utopia (if the name and place of the utopia can be named). The exact timing of something is usually a secret kept to the leaders themselves while all the other group members are expected to be in a state of perpetual readiness. Corruption and even more evil become possible with warning sign #4 because this means that the group will do ANYTHING—even violate its own precepts—in order to "get back" at the world. At this stage, the group is mobilized for action. Terrorist activity occurs in Stage (5), but by this time, the declaration of war is usually only an after-the-fact event.

> *"In reality, the only 'crime' of most 'cults' is that they hold different religious beliefs from whomever is doing the attacking."*

The Threat of Cults Is Exaggerated

Bruce A. Robinson

In the following viewpoint, Bruce A. Robinson argues that cults are not dangerous. Instead, the vast majority are new, benign religious groups that are associated with the few destructive ones to denigrate them, Robinson insists. Furthermore, he maintains that most religious groups require members to conform to specific beliefs and attempt to control behaviors across a spectrum of coercion. Harmful groups that use mind control are mostly Christian, Robinson claims, and the prevalence of deadly satanic cults is based on myths. The author is founder of Ontario Consultants on Religious Tolerance, an advocacy group based in Canada.

As you read, consider the following questions:

1. What examples does Robinson provide of Christians bring treated as cultists?

Bruce A. Robinson, "Cults (a.k.a. New Religious Movements): Introduction" and "Levels of Belief Coercion Within Religious Groups," www.religioustolerance.org, June 4, 2005, August 30, 2008. Reproduced by permission.

2. What are Robinson's allegations of Christian denominations in enforcing conformity?

3. How did belief in satanic ritual abuse spread, as told by the author?

The term "cult" is generally used as a hateful snarl word that is intended to intentionally devalue people and the new faith groups that they have chosen to follow. It tends to associate thousands of benign religious groups with the handful of destructive religious groups that have caused loss of life. The term often creates fear and loathing among the public, and contributes greatly to religious intolerance in North America. The word "cult," particularly as used by the media, carries a heavy emotional content. The term suggests that this is a group that you should detest, avoid, and fear.

Who Are the True "Cults"

In reality, the only "crime" of most "cults" is that they hold different religious beliefs from whomever is doing the attacking. For example, many conservative Christian counter-cult groups consider the Church of Jesus Christ of Latter-day Saints (LDS; the main Mormon Church) to be a cult that is tinged with Gnosticism and teaches beliefs which conflict with historic Christianity. Meanwhile, the LDS teaches that Christianity took a wrong turn in the second century CE and abandoned most of the teachings of Jesus and the apostles. They regard their own denomination as the true Christian church. Who is the cult and who is the mainline movement depends upon one's viewpoint.

History of New Religious Movements

Fear and dislike of new religious movements, coupled with increased respect for established faith groups with a long history, have been with us for at least two millennia.

- During the first century, many people in the Roman Empire rejected Christianity because it was new, and valued Judaism because of its ancient history. Today, some established religions criticize new religions simply because they are new and teach different beliefs.

- During the first century, some politicians spread rumors that Christians engaged in orgies during their love feasts, and sacrificed infants to their God. During the 1980s and early 1990s, many Christians believed that pagans, satanists, and other small religious groups engaged in orgies and ritual abuse and human sacrifice.

Meanings of the Word "Cult"

Individuals and organizations have assigned many meanings to the word "cult." The result is mass confusion:

- The counter-cult movement (CCM) classifies all non-traditional Christian faith groups as cults simply because their beliefs differ from historical Christian doctrine. The term *"cult"* has, in many ways, replaced *"heretic"* or *"nontraditional,"* or *"unconventional"* within the CCM. Examples of commonly attacked "cults" are: Seventh-day Adventists and Mormons. In this [viewpoint], we simply refer to these groups as denominations, or faith groups.

- Some Fundamentalist and other Evangelical Christians describe most non-Christian religions as cults or as satanic religions, simply because they are non-Christian. Examples are religions as different as Wicca [a religion that affirms the existence of supernatural powers and male and female deities who exist in nature] and Hinduism. We simply refer to these groups by name, as alternative religions or as faith groups.

- The largely secular anticult movement (ACM) mainly targets religious groups that make high demands on their membership. They are accused of mind control or brainwashing techniques which reduce their members to near zombielike status, who are unable to think clearly and become trapped within the group. Examples of religions targeted by the ACM are the Jehovah's Witnesses and the Two by Twos [an international, home-based religion that originated in Ireland in the nineteenth century]. Studies by mental health researchers indicate that the charges of the ACM have little or no merit. We simply refer to these groups as "high-intensity" or "high-demand" faith groups who expect great dedication from their members.

- Many information sources use the term "cult" to refer to the few destructive, doomsday religious groups whose members have been murdered or committed suicide. Examples are the Solar Temple and Heaven's Gate. We do refer to such groups as "cults."

Suggestions

We recommend that people develop a healthy skepticism when they hear someone refer to a religious group as a "cult." A new faith group may be being attacked:

- because they don't believe in the Trinity, or

- because they are non-Christian, like two-thirds of the world's population, or

- because they expect a major commitment from their membership, or

- because they are one of those rare, destructive, doomsday groups that have shown themselves to be dangerous to their membership.

" A charismatic leader, droves of elves working all the time
for nothing . . looks like cult to me ! "

"A charismatic leader, droves of elves working all the time for nothing . . . looks like cult to me!" Cartoon by Roy Delgado, www.CartoonStock.com.

We recommend that people refer to religious groups by name. If a term is needed to characterize nontraditional religious groups, we suggest a neutral phrase, like *"new religious movement,"* or *"emerging faith group."*

Levels of Belief Coercion Within Religious Groups

Essentially all religious groups require their members to conform to specific beliefs; they attempt to restrict members' behaviors to certain norms. But faith groups vary greatly in the level of demands and the degree of control that they maintain over their membership:

- At the "low control" end might be a congregation of the Unitarian Universalist Association where members are not required to believe in and follow a specific creed. They are encouraged to critically investigate all sources of spirituality for themselves. A main role of the minister and the rest of the congregation is to help each member to develop his or her own ethical and belief systems.

- The vast majority of the 1,500 or so religious organizations in North America place greater demands on their members than the Unitarian Universalist Association, but in no way can be considered high-demand groups. In the more conservative denomination, pressure for the individual to belie is a natural outgrowth of some of their theological beliefs; they often teach that only a select few who trust Jesus as Lord and Savior will be saved: The vast majority of humans will remain unsaved and spend eternity in Hell. This teaching places considerable pressure on the member to believe. Some denominations use the threat of excommunicating or disfellowshipping members in order to enforce conformity. Those members who obtain their entire spiritual, religious, and social support from the faith group frequently find exile to be very disruptive.

- At the higher end of the spectrum might be a Roman Catholic convent or monastery that requires its members to adhere to a strict schedule of sleep, work and prayer, a limited diet, poverty, celibacy, total acceptance of decisions by those in authority, etc.

- Next would be actual mind-control groups. These are often small, local, new, Christian groups who make extremely high demands on their members, and are often led by a single charismatic individual. Their total membership is quite small.

- At the "high-demand/control" end would be the destructive doomsday cults which so completely control their members that they have occasionally led many to their deaths through suicide and murder.

Actual "Mind-Control Groups"

One definition of a mind-control group is

"A religious group that engages in *extreme* spiritual, physical, mental, and emotional manipulation of its members in order to control closely their beliefs, thoughts, emotions and behavior."

The critical word here is *"extreme."*

There have existed (and continue to exist) many truly abusive mind-control groups in North America. Usually, these are headed by a single leader who uses manipulative techniques to control his/her followers. The group is tightly knit and often remains hidden unless some criminal act is discovered. Almost all are Christian (probably because about 75% of the North American population follows this religion). The anticult and counter-cult movements rarely target these groups, perhaps because their activities are not publicly known. Also, they are invariably to be local groups with a small membership. They are virtually undetectable unless some criminal activity brings them to the attention of the police and press.

Sometimes these mind-control groups become known because of their use of physical abuse, particularly of children. A massive study of child abuse funded by the US federal government did uncover a troubling level of what they called *"religion-related abuse."* Much of this abuse probably occurs within mind-control cults. The study identified three main forms of child abuse:

- psychological and physical abuse during exorcisms

- unreasonably harsh corporal punishment of children due to religiously influenced child-raising beliefs

- withholding needed medical attention from children in favor of prayer

During 1995, two instances of unintentional deaths during exorcisms were widely publicized in North America. One occurred in California; the other in Ontario, Canada. Similar deaths have been extensively published since, at the rate of about one per year. One can reasonably assume that there was much unreported abuse during exorcisms that did not lead to death of the victim. Accounts of children needlessly dying of treatable diseases surface from time to time in which the church group required that prayer be used in place of medical intervention.

A Nonexistent Mind-Control Cult

There is one group that up to 90% of Americans believe exist: an intergenerational, underground, international satanic conspiracy which kidnaps children, abuses them physically and sexually, ritually kills them, eats their flesh and drinks their blood. This is perhaps the longest-lasting urban folk tale in existence, having been circulating since about the 2nd century CE. There are a whole range of myths that have arisen about these groups: They allegedly keep thousands of women in concentration camps to generate babies for sacrifice; they kill about 50,000 infants in the United States every year; their rituals are inverted, sacrilegious parodies on Christian religious practices, etc.

Belief in satanic ritual abuse (SRA) became widespread in the 1980s, partly triggered by the publishing of the book *Michelle Remembers*. Many therapists began experimenting with recovered memory therapy, which generated false "memories" of abusive events in clients' childhoods. Some of these memories reinforced beliefs about SRA. By the mid-1990s, due to the lack of physical evidence of childhood abuse, beliefs in SRA declined.

No hard evidence has ever been found to support any of these beliefs. Many of the myths are traceable to the "burning times" during the late Middle Ages and Renaissance, when many tens of thousands of people suspected of selling their souls to Satan were routinely rounded up, tortured and executed.

> *"In a country with 183,000 officially reg-*
> *istered religious organisations—and*
> *perhaps thousands of unregistered*
> *ones—how many of them exert total*
> *control over believers, and how many*
> *could turn nasty?"*

Cults Are a Serious Threat in Japan

Leo Lewis

Leo Lewis is the Asian business correspondent for the Times *of London and contributor to* Monocle *magazine. In the following viewpoint, Lewis writes that Japan is vulnerable to cultism because of the affinity for religion in its culture and thousands of small faith groups. Experts on cult behavior, he points out, warn that group psychology and religious beliefs increase the Japanese population's susceptibility to irrational behavior and thought control. As an example, Lewis describes how the illogical beliefs of the Kigenkai cult, a registered religion in the country, led to the murder of an elderly member and placed other members' health in jeopardy.*

As you read, consider the following questions:

1. What is the Kigensui, as described by the author?

2. What is at the root of the cult problem in Japan, as stated by Shoko Egawa?

3. How did the Kigenkai cult respond to a member's stomach ailments, as told by the author?

It was another quiet autumn night at the Yoshinozushi restaurant on the deserted main drag of Komoro. Once the place had thronged with fans of its Kyoto-style sweet sushi, but a few years ago they had suddenly vanished: what was known in town as the "cult's sushi shop" was empty.

The owner, 63-year-old Motoko Okuno, was preparing to close at 11pm when she allegedly received an abrupt summons from the leaders of the cult that had brainwashed her for decades: Come immediately to our headquarters. The message was a death sentence.

When she arrived at the opulent facilities of the Kigenkai cult, perched on the hill above Komoro, Motoko was shown into a room filled with dozens of familiar faces: women, young and old, with whom she had eaten, drunk and prayed for many years. The men had already been sent away.

Her 26-year-old daughter, Michiko, was there, her son-in-law too. Michiko, the leaders told her, had transgressed the Kigenkai ("Era-society") code. Her crime was that she had jokingly shown a condom to the "Great Deity's" granddaughter, and told her that it was a protective amulet that would guarantee prosperity. As a punishment, Michiko had been forced to wear a bin bag plastered in condoms, and was beaten up by cult members.

Now, Motoko was told, she too must pay for her daughter's crimes. A blow to her back knocked her to the floor. She writhed in pain as the women pounded her with a deadly hail of fists and feet.

As the agony stretched on for nearly an hour, a fake gun was rammed into her mouth and her face caked in chalk by way of ritualistic humiliation. To complete the shaming, members rode on Motoko's back, grabbing handfuls of her hair as "reins".

In the background, police claim, orders were given to the 50-strong female mob by Yasuko Kubota, the 49-year-old daughter of the guru who had founded the Shinto-based Ki-genkai cult in 1970. It is a version of events strongly denied by Kubota herself.

The guru was a man Motoko had devoted her life to but whose teachings, since his death five years ago [in 2002], have become twisted beyond recognition.

The guru had always liked Motoko, and it was a favouritism that had caused a rift within the cult.

Kubota's orders, say police, were calculated to heighten the victim's pain: "Stamp on the inside of her thighs," she commanded, and the cult's enraged flock obeyed. Women in their eighties looked on; girls as young as 15 were told to join in or they could never hope to be "children of the gods".

As the orgy of violence subsided, Motoko lay motionless on the floor.

Somebody produced a bottle of Kigensui—the "magical" water sold to cult followers for Y60,000 (£300) per litre— which, they believed, was capable of curing every known ailment.

Motoko's body and mouth was liberally splashed with this supposed elixir of life, but, at the critical moment, its much vaunted powers were nowhere to be seen. Motoko was dead.

Motoko's body was taken secretly back to the sushi shop, and the place wrecked to make it look as if she had died in a domestic fight. In fear of further reprisal by the cult, Motoko's daughter and husband told the police that they had killed her accidentally. Their confessions were quickly dismissed as flimsy inventions. A fortnight later, 21 cult members were arrested for the killing: the youngest was 15, the oldest 81.

By last week [in November 2007] 15 of those women, including Kubota herself, had been officially charged with injury leading to death, and two with the attempted cover-up. But even police admit that the deeper mystery of the Kigenkai remains unsolved. How did entire families become sucked into its belief system? Why was there such a high proportion of women members involved in the beating? Had there, as the townspeople of Komoro mutter, been deaths before that had been more successfully covered up?

"There are things we still do not know and we are still investigating," said one senior Komoro police officer. "We don't exactly know why this particular family was targeted, or why the woman was killed for something her daughter was accused of." There are enough gaps in the case to trouble even the National Police Agency 100 miles away in Tokyo: Was this an ultra-rare glimpse into a large, sinister sect with tentacles across Japan or just a final death spasm of a clique on the edge of extinction?

A "Fertile Paddy Field" of Cultism

The Kigenkai incident has provoked uncomfortable soul-searching as people wonder whether Japan, for all its reputation as an irreligious technoscape, is in fact a "fertile paddy field" of cultism. In a country with 183,000 officially registered religious organisations—and perhaps thousands of unregistered ones—how many of them exert total control over believers, and how many could turn nasty?

Japanese experts on cult behaviour have long warned of the dangers posed by ignoring the country's "hidden" affinity for religion and the capacity for small religious groups to grow invisibly yet epidemically into powerful forces of thought control.

Shoko Egawa, an expert on cultism, described Japan as especially susceptible to cultism: "When something is going on in a closed space where group psychology and religious belief work together, people's behaviour will eventually stop being led by rational thought," she said.

Kigenkai, as an officially registered religion, operates virtually tax free. "The government and local authorities examine the group when they issue approvals, but they don't examine the organisations ever again. They don't even know what to examine. This is the root of the whole problem," she said.

Even for the nonexpert residents of sleepy Komoro, tucked away among the beautiful mountain forests of Nagano, the death of Motoko was perhaps not totally unexpected. For more than 30 years, the townspeople had watched as the Kigenkai cult grew more and more eccentric, expanded in size and wealth, and drew hundreds of followers from elsewhere in Japan.

Tempting Curiosity

Today, eerily silent since the October arrests, the sprawling headquarters of the cult rise from the hill above Komoro in sparkling contrast with the decaying shabbiness of the town below. It is enough to tempt any resident's curiosity.

For Komoro itself is one of Japan's slowly dying towns—a place that once bustled with tourists and local craftsmen but which now creaks through life on the front line of the national ageing crisis. The only visible inhabitants are elderly, and in the toy shop the lurid robots on display in the window are dulled with dust. Komoro's shopping streets are mostly shuttered: Any stores still in business seem far too quiet to survive much longer.

But the Kigenkai headquarters gleam with opulence. Straddling a winding hill-road, the large, ice-white buildings of the cult would not be out of place in the wealthiest districts of Tokyo.

Gold plaques bearing the seal of the Yamato dynasty adorn the eaves, and everything is meticulously clean.

Halfway towards the main shrine, we are stopped by a guard: Any further progress requires a series of formal bows and hand-claps towards a pair of stone statues flanking the central building.

It is not just the shrine and the buildings that give the Kigenkai its aura of mystery, say residents. There were those times when cult members paraded through town and dumped vast quantities of fish and fruit into the local river. Or there was the ritual where zealots dug a huge hole in the side of Mount Asama and threw in votive offerings of fried tofu slices to appease the fox-god. To nearby residents' consternation, the offering succeeded chiefly in attracting actual foxes—along with an unwanted flock of jungle crows and a plague of mice.

Long-term residents of Komoro describe decades of such bizarre events, all stemming from the arrival in the mid-1960s of Kensuke Matsui, an outsider from Yokohama who wore tattered military fatigues, and claimed to be the reincarnation of Yamato Takeru No Mikoto—the prince of the ancient Yamato dynasty. He also claimed to be an exorcist and a healer. And, to everyone's surprise, plenty of local people believed him.

One of them was Mikiko Koike (not her real name), a 68-year-old storekeeper who managed to escape the cult's clutches some years ago, but lives in constant fear that disciples will one day come to her shop and dish out a fatal punishment lynching.

"I joined because of the headaches," she says. "My husband joined because I was a member, and the rest of the family then had to join because we were both members." Fighting back tears, Mikiko describes blinding headaches that followed the birth of her son. Doctors whom she visited were unable to treat the migraines, and eventually, in desperation she turned to Matsui—the proto-guru who was, at this stage, still calling himself "the teacher". Mikiko's problem, according to the diagnosis, was that she had walked through the ceremonial Torii gates of a Shinto shrine in Kyoto while her baby was still too

Cultic Behaviors Are Embedded in Japanese Culture

The therapeutic or "divine" messages of the cult, which are meant to induce self-reconstruction, are deeply embedded in Japanese culture, particularly in its moral values. At the same time, they hyperbolize what the average Japanese would believe and practice. This is why outsiders—nonmember Japanese—tend to be ambivalent toward the cult: On the one hand, they are impressed with the strong faith and moral commitment exhibited by the cult members; but on the other, they find the members' behavior odd, eccentric, or even "insane."

Takie Sugiyama Lebra and William P. Lebra, eds.,
Japanese Culture and Behavior: Selected Readings.
Honolulu: University of Hawaii Press, 1986.

young. He absolved her of the sin and the headaches stopped immediately. "That was when I started to believe," she whispers sadly.

The Great Deity

For the first few years, she continues, the Kigenkai was a friendly affair. Matsui lived in the town with everyone else and disciples could drop in on him at any time. Offerings were made at a small shrine in his house and his behaviour was modest. But in 1970, the idyll ended.

"Things had started to turn before 1970, but it all changed when the Kigenkai became officially recognised as a religion by the ministry of education and moved up the hill," says Mikiko. "That was when he started selling the Kigensui water and people began sending him envelopes full of cash. Word spread across the country and we heard that membership numbers were into the thousands." She produces an empty bottle of the Kigensui water, carefully kept for 20 years in its elegant lacquered box, and confides her long-standing doubt that the expensive "panacea" was anything more than tap water.

"Suddenly, Matsui was no longer 'the teacher,' but wanted to be known as the 'Great Deity,'" she says. "We could no longer just go to see him and he started to drive around in very expensive cars. You could really feel the influence of the whole thing dividing Komoro—everyone knew exactly who was in the Kigenkai and who wasn't."

As the guru's power grew, so too did the scope of his festivals. On one occasion, say local people, around 5,000 uniformed cult members descended on the town to celebrate the birth of the "second messiah"—the guru's daughter who would one day succeed him as the leader of the now wealthy sect. Some years later, on her first day at primary school, the daughter emerged from a crimson Rolls-Royce from which a red carpet was unfurled by an obliging team of zealots.

Mikiko and her husband, though completely under the guru's spell at the time, found some of the antics blush worthy. "It was embarrassing to go into a supermarket to buy ten kilos of fried tofu. Everyone knew two people couldn't eat that much, so they instantly knew we were Kigenkai members and that the tofu was destined to be thrown into the river. We even drove to the river at night so nobody would see us wasting all that food," she says.

Shaken to the Core

But, adds Mikiko, it was the Kigensui that undid the whole affair. As Matsui's teachings grew ever more doctrinaire, so too did his insistence that believers rely entirely on the water for all medical needs. Any trip to a mainstream doctor would be punished.

When she started suffering from acute stomach pains, Mikiko persevered with drinking the water. The elixir did nothing and eventually her husband, Takeo, intervened. "I was a member of the Kigenkai, of course, but I could see that she was genuinely ill," he says. "Her parents were also members and insisted that she was not taken to a real doctor, and anyway, we were terrified that people would see us going to the local hospital and report us to the Great Deity." Eventually, Mikiko was smuggled out to a hospital in another town, where a doctor instantly diagnosed cancer. Unable to break free from the guru's mental hold over her, she told him what the doctor had said.

Her prescription was more Kigensui water. If she did anything else, the guru said, Mikiko's shop would go bankrupt and she would die. A month or so later, at death's door, she returned to the real doctor who removed three-quarters of her stomach in an emergency operation. "That was when I stopped believing," she whispers.

But Mikiko and her husband were not alone. The faith of thousands of Kigenkai members was shaken to the core when, in 2002, the water's mystical powers were once again found wanting and the guru himself died of pancreatic cancer. Thousands of members—mostly living outside Komoro itself, are thought to have abandoned their faith in the years that followed, but the cult itself did not die.

Former believers say that the Kigenkai, which is thought to have been taken over by the guru's daughter, became ever more fierce in its attempts to control the zealots as membership—and income—bled away. The fatal beating of Mrs Okuno, say those who have escaped the cult's tendrils, was a tragedy waiting to happen.

> "[The Children of God] may well claim they no longer practise the brutal physical punishment or adult-child sex, but how does this rectify the crimes that were committed against us and so many other innocent children?"

Some Cults Are Sexually Abusive

Celeste Jones, Kristina Jones, and Juliana Buhring

Celeste Jones is a former cult member. She wrote Not Without My Sister: The True Story of Three Girls Violated and Betrayed *with her sister Kristina Jones and Juliana Buhring, another former cult member. In the following viewpoint excerpted from* Not Without My Sister, *Jones retells a childhood of sexual abuse in a cult that decreed sex as the highest expression of love. Born to parents in the Children of God, a religious organization also once known as the Family of Love and known today as the Family International, she claims to have been sexually groomed at an early age and arranged to have sex with boys and adult men before reaching adolescence. Not knowing life outside of the cult, Jones says she remained with the Children of God until adulthood—and even spoke against the allegations of sexual abuse against the cult—until she escaped.*

Celeste Jones, Kristina Jones, and Juliana Buhring, *Not Without My Sister*, Harper-Elements, 2007. © 2007 Celeste Jones and Kristina Jones. Reproduced by permission.

As you read, consider the following questions:

1. As stated by Jones, what was she shown as a child in communal school?

2. How does Jones claim to have been punished after speaking out against being sexually abused in the cult?

3. In her words, why did Jones finally escape the Children of God?

There is an old, grainy home video from my childhood which I sometimes sit down to watch and which never fails to make me shudder. It starts innocently enough—I am six years old, a small, slim, dark-haired child dancing to pipe music for the camera. But this is no ordinary family movie.

As the camera focuses, you can see that I am naked, dancing behind a white veil.

I remember filming the video as if it was yesterday—and how the man "directing" it asked me to rub my bottom and to wriggle for the camera. The tragedy is that already at that age I had been forced to become sexualised. Quite simply, sexual grooming was an everyday part of my life.

I was born to ordinary, middle-class English parents, and by rights I should have enjoyed a perfectly normal childhood. But my parents—a former public schoolboy and rather naive young teenage girl—were members of the sinister Children of God cult [also once known by the name the Family of Love and currently known as the Family International], in which adult orgies and sex between adults and children were considered the highest expression of love.

Sickeningly, the cult leader David Berg, or 'Mo' as he called himself, claimed that God intended everyone to become part of a sexual experience. The result was a childhood of abuse and pain.

The Highest Expression of Love

It should have been so different. My father, Christopher Jones, was born in December 1951, the son of a British army officer. Educated at public school in Cheltenham, he studied drama at Rose Bruford College and joined the Children of God in 1973.

My mother Rebecca was born in 1957 and had a secure upbringing in the south of England. Her father was a civil engineer and her mother a devoted housewife. Rebecca was recruited during a visit to her school by the Children of God when she was just 16, and married our father a year later in 1974.

I was born on January 29, 1975, and we were sent to join a commune in Bombay which was part of the cult, and where my sister Kristina was born 18 months later.

Months later, Berg decreed that sex was the highest expression of love, and giving it was called "sharing".

Both my parents started sharing their bodies with others—but after the birth of my brother David in April 1978, Mum became increasingly depressed.

When she met another family member, Joshua, she decided to return to England with Kristina and David. "But I insisted on keeping you," Dad would tell me, "you're my girl."

I was just three years old when my mum left. When I was five, my father announced that he had fallen for our young German nanny Serena, who became my stepmother.

We lived in a commune known as Loveville, led by Paul Péloquin and his wife Marianne.

Discipline was strict. Reveille was at 7.30am, and after breakfast, I'd go to our communal school. We were shown illustrated stories which were often filled with scenes of explicit sex, nudity or gruesome demons.

When I was six, Berg requested the women to dance naked for him on the video which I still have today. I watched the women, then the other girls, strip and dance. Then a white veil was tied around my neck, which I was supposed to take off during the dance, and Paul gave directions from behind the camera: "Wiggle nicely and rub your bottom, honey."

I simply copied the motions I had seen the adult women perform earlier. "Good, very good! Now blow kisses," he said. Watching it now makes me feel physically sick. Nude pictures were taken of us girls on a regular basis and sent to Berg.

Sex was completely open and transparent in our world. The adults had no inhibitions about making love in front of us and actively encouraged us to explore our bodies.

My father never did anything to me in a sexual way but his friend Soloman, a Londoner, would ask me to dance for him naked in his bedroom. "You're so sexy!" he would say.

One man, Manuel, helped teach us our dance routines. As I slept in a caravan one night with my friends, he woke me, pulled down my pants and started kissing me.

"This is how the adult women do it," he explained. I was about seven years old and was terrified. I just wanted to scream, but nothing came out. When I watched the adults having sex, they seemed to enjoy it, so why didn't I?

Once a week, our commune would gather for a dance night, and the adults—all those over the age of 12—paired off for sex.

Meanwhile, during the day, everything would stop for so-called "Cuddle Time"—a euphemism for group sex.

I remember lying horrified in the clutches of my teacher, Johnny Appleseed (some of the cult members took stupid, folksy names), while other adults were having sex around us. When he finished assaulting me, he said a prayer as I lay in terror.

In June 1981, my half-sister Juliana was born to my father and Serena. We moved to a commune and during one sermon, the leader stripped off his clothes. Everyone, including the children, obediently followed.

Everyone sat together naked, arms around each other, then the men were instructed to take a sip from the communal cup and pass it on to the mouth of their female partner. When the wine came round, my adult partner took a gulp and then fixed his mouth on mine. It was disgusting.

Bizarre Missives and Sinister Orders

In the commune, I was forever scared of being singled out for punishment. Once, when I angered the leader, Paul, he singled me out for public humiliation—telling me to hold out my hand and raining down blow after blow on it. The pain was so excruciating, I could barely move my wrist for a week.

Around that time, we moved to a communal house rented by the sect and were ordered to change our names—possibly because the leaders wanted us to be untraceable by our families in England. I chose Rebecca—Dad renamed himself Happy, which I thought was very odd.

Families were separated all the time. When I was eight, the leaders decided to keep me apart from Dad, and only let me see him once a week, while other couples helped to raise me.

Can you begin to imagine how distressing that was for a little girl who had already been ripped away from her mother?

All the while, bizarre missives continued to spew forth from the cult leader.

Berg decided we were all to use spoons, instead of forks. We could not use black pepper, women could not wear jeans, and men replaced their briefs with boxer shorts just because he expressed his dislike for them. Fruit and vegetables had to be soaked in salt water for 20 minutes—which made them taste awful.

Other orders were far more sinister. Paul Péloquin announced during one meeting that all adults had to write down in order of preference who they would like to be on the "date schedule"—in other words, who they wished to have sex with.

When I was 11 years old, Paul decided that my best friend Armi and I had to have sex with two boys, Patrick and Nicki, aged 12 and nine. This was to happen once a week.

Armi and I were also "scheduled" with the adult men—sex with men old enough to be my father.

It was a horrific assault on my prepubescent body, but I had to bear it; I was powerless to stop it. Now, when I look back at the terrible things that were done to me, I see that my father should have done something to stop it, but he didn't.

How could a man stand by while his 11-year-old daughter was effectively raped by another man?

The former Fleetwood Mac band member Jeremy Spencer was a member of the cult. On the regular dates we had, he would play a tape of saxophone music. The routine was, by now, familiar—undress, pray, kiss and then perform lewd acts for him.

One night, a short, fat, bald man called Eman came into my room. I simply couldn't bear the thought of having sex with him, and I ran to the one adult I hoped might save me—my schoolteacher Sally.

"He's horrible and disgusting," I told her.

"Sweetie, sometimes it can be difficult to share," she replied, "but God gives us the strength to do it. Why don't we pray together?"

I listened in disgust to her prayer, feeling betrayed and helpless—and was led back to this pervert's room. I don't know how long his assault lasted, but it gave me nightmares for years.

I never thought of telling Dad how I felt, especially after one evening when I walked in on him lying on the bed half-dressed with my 11-year-old friend Armi. Years later, he claimed that this young child had made a move on him. He always insisted that nothing sexual had happened.

The thought of that encounter deeply disturbed me. We never talked about any of my sexual experiences, nor did he ask me.

The Loyalty Test

Transparent as it may seem to those not in a cult, the expectation that true followers will demonstrate their loyalty is an effective tool for manipulating cult members. The more a leader demands, the more power he gets. Soon he intrudes and controls every aspect of life. The rationale is that nothing is too sacred to withhold from the leader. Giving oneself, and sometimes even one's children, is viewed as a noble sacrifice. Physical violence and sexual abuse are incorporated into elaborate rituals in some cults, where these activities are endowed with mystical or magical meanings. In some cults, the testing of loyalty may be done in a sexually sadistic manner, further debilitating the follower and increasing personal confusion and dependency on the leader.

Janja Lalich, "Dominance and Submission:
The Psychosexual Exploitation of Women in Cults,"
Cultic Studies Journal, vol. 14, no. 1, 1997, p. 12.

I spent most of my time with my foster parents, Patience and Michael. But when Michael demanded sex from me and I complained to the leaders, I was forced to write endless letters of repentance.

Apart for Almost 15 Years

In 1987, I was taken to a Teen Training Camp, where we were given questionnaires and told to answer honestly.

I detailed the traumatic sexual experiences I had suffered, and as a result was "sentenced" to a month in isolation, not allowed to talk to anyone else and given only soup and water for three days. The hunger pains were my only company as I was confined in a small room set apart from everyone else.

At 14, I learned that my mother and 12-year-old sister Kristina—whom I had not seen for many years—had left the cult. Kristina had been sexually abused from the age of three by my mother's second partner Joshua, and then other men from the cult.

When my mother finally realised just how badly her daughter had been abused, she found the courage to flee to England, along with her youngest five children.

Then, on my 18th birthday, some of the cult leaders told me that Mum and Kristina were causing a media storm in England, appearing on television and speaking out against the cult. They told me I was to be 'media trained' and then sent to England to meet them and defuse the situation.

My heart began beating faster at the thought of meeting Mum—and the night before I flew home, I could hardly sleep.

We were brought together at a house in North London. Mum walked into the room and the childhood image I had carried in my head starkly contrasted with the woman that stood in front of me.

She had put on weight—and she was a stranger. I had no idea what to say to her except for "Hi, Mum." It was only when I uttered that word that she kissed me.

"You've grown," she smiled. "What shoe size are you?" I had no idea.

I didn't even know how to react to a mother overcome with emotion at seeing the young daughter she had been apart from for almost 15 years.

"I want you to know that I never wanted to leave you," Mum said, and burst into tears. I was unsure how to respond. I should have gone to hug her, but instead I sat awkwardly in front of her.

After lunch, Mum introduced me to my sister Kristina, brother David and my grandparents—I was greeted with hugs, kisses and questions and I so wanted to get to know them better.

The leaders of the cult who had accompanied me made me draft an affidavit stating that I hadn't been abused as a child. Lying on a desk, I found another affidavit which Kristina had written, saying she had been abused from the age of three by grown men including her stepfather.

I felt physically sick and I knew instantly that she wasn't lying because I had suffered the same abuse. But I was too scared to leave the Family—it was the only world I knew.

Over the next year and a half, I appeared on a number of television programmes, including Sky News and the BBC, to deny the stories my mother and Kristina were openly talking about.

After a few days, I flew back to the cult. I know people will find it hard to believe that I wanted to go back to that, but I was so indoctrinated that I knew no other way.

A Life-Changing Event

It was to be several years before a life-changing event made me realize I had to escape. I fell pregnant by a man named Vince who was in the cult—I'd never used any contraception—and my daughter Cherie was born on August 9, 1998.

When she was just a few weeks old I began to be horrified at the debauchery that was still raging around me. I constantly suffered flashbacks to the abuse I'd suffered and I knew I could never allow my own daughter to suffer the same fate.

I flew back to England having saved the money for my fare from the secretarial job the cult had allowed me to do. Back in Britain, I joyfully joined my mother and Kristina.

Since then, I have slowly rebuilt my life. I worked as a volunteer for the charity Parentline Plus, and graduated from Nottingham Trent University in 2006 with a degree in psychology and education.

I live with my daughter in Somerset, where I am pursuing a career as a clinical psychologist.

Together, we have founded an organisation called RISE International which works to protect children from all forms of abuse in isolated and/or extremist cults.

The leaders of the Children of God continue to live in hiding, and have never accepted responsibility or shown remorse for those hurt by their wicked doctrines.

They call us liars, and they may well claim they no longer practise the brutal physical punishment or adult-child sex, but how does this rectify the crimes that were committed against us and so many other innocent children?

| *"This is not about consenting adults.*
My position is it is sexual slavery."

Polygamist Cults Threaten Women and Girls

Carolyn Jessop, as told to Luiza Ch. Savage

Carolyn Jessop is a former member of the Fundamentalist Church of Jesus Christ of Latter-day Saints (FLDS) and author of the books Escape *and* Triumph: Life After the Cult—A Survivor's Lessons. *Luiza Ch. Savage is the Washington bureau chief for* Maclean's. *In the following viewpoint, Jessop asserts that polygamist groups systematically abuse women and children. She accuses the FLDS of marrying girls as young as twelve to men with multiple wives, in which underage marriages facilitate sexual assault. Women are also prevented from leaving the groups through numerous tactics, Jessop says, from constant surveillance to the denial of spousal support and property. Therefore, she supports anti-polygamist legislation to stop the violation of children's rights in these groups.*

As you read, consider the following questions:

1. Why isn't the sexual assault of minors that occurs in polygamist groups typical of other types of sexual assault, as alleged by Jessop?

Carolyn Jessop, interviewed by Luiza Ch. Savage, "On Polygamy, Child Brides, and Why the Stakes in BC Are So High: Carolyn Jessop in Conversation with Luiza Ch. Savage," *Maclean's*, vol. 124, April 4, 2011, p. 12. Reproduced by permission.

2. According to Jessop, how are women physically prevented from leaving polygamist communities?

3. Why does Jessop oppose the strike down of Canada's anti-polygamy laws?

Carolyn Jessop, 43, was born in the U.S. into a radical polygamist cult, the Fundamentalist Church of Jesus Christ of Latter-day Saints (FLDS). At 18, she became the fourth wife of a 50-year-old man and bore eight children. She recounts the abuses she endured and her harrowing flight in a book, *Escape*. She recently testified before the Supreme Court of British Columbia, which is considering whether polygamy laws violate religious freedom under the Charter [referring to the Canadian Charter of Rights and Freedoms] and whether they can be used to prosecute FLDS leaders in Bountiful, B.C.

[Luiza Ch. Savage:] Critics of anti-polygamy laws say that the state should not interfere with the religious beliefs or lifestyle decisions of consenting adults. Do you agree?

[Carolyn Jessop:] This is not about consenting adults. My position is it is sexual slavery. I was never asked. I was told what I was going to do. My husband Merril never asked me to marry him. The purpose of marriage is not to fall in love but to provide righteous children. They say it's a victimless crime. I have not seen a polygamous situation that is not abusive to someone in the relationship.

Systematic Abuse

Ironically, you describe your husband, who had more than a dozen wives and 54 children, as emotionally monogamous.

If a man gets many wives, he'll find one he has chemistry with. Once they fall in love, things get difficult for the other women. If he's not having sex with you, your status in the family goes down. When he shuts you out, they know you are just a prime target for whatever abuse they want to throw at you because he won't protect you or your kids.

Did you witness child abuse?

Systematic abuse. There is a lot of violence toward kids. Merril did a lot of water torture on his babies.

What is water torture?

The concept is that you have to break a child's will before the age of 2. If you don't, you'll never be able to control them at the level that their salvation depends on. A baby may be crying because it is hungry. They would take the baby and spank it to really get it going. Then they hold the baby faceup under cold running water for 30 seconds, and as soon as it gets its breath and starts crying, they'd spank it again. A session like that could last an hour until the baby quits fighting from fatigue. That can happen frequently until the parent feels the baby is sufficiently broken.

And you say the community was rife with child sexual abuse?

This isn't a typical sexual assault of a minor. Parents are involved in this. That's what makes it so egregious. Underage marriage is a conspiracy to have sex with minors. The parents are involved, the grandparents, the aunts and uncles. The options the girls have for help and relief from those crimes— they virtually have none.

The RCMP [Royal Canadian Mounted Police] are now investigating evidence that cult members were smuggling Canadian girls as young as 12 to marry men in the U.S. One of them ended up being given to your husband.

Back in 2008, when they did the raids at the Yearning for Zion Ranch in Texas [referring to a raid by Texas law enforcement officers who removed more than 500 women and children from the compound after an alleged claim of physical and sexual abuse by one of its female members], three of the minors that had been sexually assaulted under the pretense of marriage and didn't know where their parents were, were from Canada. They were brought into the States by the parents, given to [FLDS leader] Warren Jeffs on a silver platter and abandoned. The investigator in Texas, Angie Voss, sent a report to Canada, saying [they had] three girls who were trafficked [there] for the purposes of sex. That got lost in the system and nothing was ever done. As far as I know, they are still in the U.S. Merril married another Canadian girl who was 16 at the time.

What happens to boys when all the girls are married off to the old men of the church?

Boys are disposable. It's simple math. They excommunicate them. They dump a 13-year-old boy on the street, in a big city, and tell him they never want to see him again because he has been turned to the temptations of Satan. There are crimes committed against children in these groups that if committed in a regular household, the family would lose their children.

Huge Obstacles in Leaving

Why not just leave?

Getting out of the community is a huge obstacle. You are not free to say, "Oh, I don't want to do this anymore." They hunt you down. They take you back and put you under 24-hour surveillance, take your kids away and tell you that you can't see them again.

What obstacles did you face?

The first was legal: How do you get legal custody of your kids? Merril hired an attorney who was paid around $1 million. Family attorneys would not touch my case because they would be taking on a cult, and they only did family law. I didn't have any money. My attorney, Lisa Jones, said it was the most stressful case in her career. She did it as a favour to the state attorney general of Utah, who told her we cannot lose. If we lose, no other woman will ever come forward. I was the first one to ever leave the FLDS and get legal custody of all my children and get all of them out. Another problem a woman has is the fact that we are in an illegal lifestyle. When I went into court to fight for my kids, it was viewed as two criminals fighting over the kids. I didn't get any advantages that women would get who are leaving an abusive situation.

Why didn't you have any money?

My husband had a home worth more than $1 million—it was 17,000 square feet for seven wives and 30-some kids. I had no claim, even though I worked as a teacher and all my money contributed to that home. But it was all in a church-controlled trust. He had other assets such as construction equipment that he put in the name of other members. It was a fraudulent transfer and the state could have traced it back to him, but they didn't want to do that. My case didn't fit the simple system where he gets a paycheque and you garnish it for child support. He would have had to give support for eight kids and one with a severe disability and in critical condition with cancer. That's one of the problems with polygamy. Women don't have any protection from financial abuse. He was flying around in a private jet and I was in a homeless shelter.

When you escaped, you discovered he had run up debts in your name.

He was using my name to finance different things—credit cards, construction equipment. When I left, he stopped paying. I didn't know what I owed. He legally got away without paying child support and pushed me into bankruptcy, and it did not hurt him because we were not legally married. Harrison, my 11-year-old disabled son, at the time was 4. He needed 24-hour-a-day care. That forced me onto welfare.

How are women prevented from physically leaving the community you were in, on the Arizona-Utah border?

The men work construction and are gone during the week. They are not there to watch their wives. They don't want her taking her kids to go to town but it's not practical to leave a woman with a lot of little kids with no transportation. So they leave her a clunker that's unlicensed and uninsured to make sure that she cannot leave the community. The minute I start driving outside of the community, they know I'm leaving without permission. It's like driving a marked car.

Why not go to the police?

The cops are members of the cult. Merril would have called and said, 'My wife is leaving and you'd better get over and stop her.' I tried to call a cop outside of the community; they said we don't have jurisdiction there.

What made you finally decide to leave?

It was a combination of how critical things were becoming because Warren Jeffs had become the prophet and he was preaching the "lifting up." I could see he was starting to program us for a mass suicide. I was also afraid for the safety of my daughter, who was turning 14 and I knew Warren wanted to marry her. The other factor was my disabled son. I was having hell on wheels getting him treatment, keeping him alive.

The Need for Anti-Polygamy Laws

What do you think would happen if courts strike down Canada's anti-polygamy law?

It could have a devastating impact. It would push the legalization of polygamy into the U.S. It would help mainstream that lifestyle. We want to see specific legislation to go after specific crimes they are committing, such as educational neglect of children, medical neglect, in addition to sexual assault. If Canada says this is legal, there probably won't be legislation to deal with these crimes.

You tell U.S. audiences Canada represents "hope" because of the potential for prosecutions of leaders of a branch of the FLDS in Bountiful, who had many underage brides.

Canada presents a hope to me for two reasons. They are looking very seriously at crimes within the polygamous community. The other encouraging thing is because they are looking at a polygamist population of fewer than 2,000 people, dealing with the situation is more feasible. In Utah we have 80,000. If Canada prosecutes, it would put serious heat on Utah.

What do you think the Canadian government should do?

They should pass specific legislation. If children are born into it, you can't take away all their Charter rights in the name of freedom of religion. Regardless of what you believe, you don't have a right to deprive a child of all their other rights. You couldn't just take girls over international lines and give them over to sexual abuse when they are 12. You can open the door to freedom for people who are trapped. It's not about consenting adults. There are children there.

> *"Polygamy, or more correctly, poly-*
> *gyny—the marriage of multiple women*
> *to one man—not only has a long and*
> *noble tradition throughout world his-*
> *tory, but it is currently practiced in*
> *more countries than strict monogamy*
> *is."*

The Practice of Polygamy Is Defensible

Jacob Hodgen

In the following viewpoint, Jacob Hodgen defends the practice of polygamy. He claims that plural marriage is not based on sexual pleasure, but is considered by numerous religions as a practical approach to raising families. Moreover, the author suggests, monogamy is unnatural and results in widespread divorce and infidelity. Hodgen calls on Mormons to embrace their polygamist origins, given their preaching of plural marriage in heaven, its acceptance by spiritual leaders, and its existence throughout history. Hodgen is a product manager in information technology and former senior columnist and managing editor of Utah Stories.

Jacob Hodgen, "In Defense of Polygamy," *Utah Stories*, August 2, 2010. Reproduced by permission.

As you read, consider the following questions:

1. Why is polygamous marriage supported by scripture and approved by God, in Hodgen's view?

2. Why is polygamous marriage encouraged in Malaysia, as told by Hodgen?

3. What does Dorothy Allred Solomon state about polygamy in fundamentalist households?

The truth is that nothing could be more "traditional family values" than the practice of plural marriage. Polygamy, or more correctly, polygyny—the marriage of multiple women to one man—not only has a long and noble tradition throughout world history, but it is currently practiced in more countries than strict monogamy is. With all the recent talk in Utah of getting back to America's Christian roots, there is really only one defensible position on polygamy, and everyone is in agreement.

Strange Bedfellows: Support for Polygamy Is Bipartisan and Growing

Whether you are Christian, Muslim, or Hindu, you can rest assured that plural marriage is based on the firm foundation of written scripture and has the full approval of God. Ancient king-prophets such as the biblical patriarch Jacob, Islamic founder Muhammad, and the god Vishnu all famously had numerous wives.

Polygamy is not at all about sexual gratification but is viewed as a convenient and pragmatic approach to raising a family by the faithful. In Malaysia, for example, the national Islamic Party calls for men to generously practice polygamous marriage with single mothers instead of just exclusively with "young virgin girls."

Some modern philosophers, such as Friedrich Engels, believed that monogamy is oppressive. Considering contemporary divorce and infidelity rates, numerous scientists have also concluded that only having one sexual partner is highly unnatural.

On the left, even the ACLU [American Civil Liberties Union] has supported polygamy. "Talking to Utah's polygamists is like talking to gays and lesbians who really want the right to live their lives, and not live in fear because of whom they love," said Utah [ACLU legal] director Stephen Clark. "So certainly that kind of privacy expectation is something the ACLU is committed to protecting."

The Far Right also agrees: Utah's Libertarian candidate for governor, Andrew McCullough, supports the decriminalization of both bigamy and gay marriage.

Even local celebrity and polygamy exposé author Dorothy Allred Solomon, the 28th of 48 children in a fundamentalist household, still endorses plural marriage. Though her father was murdered by a rival polygamist and she has since converted to the mainstream LDS [Church of Jesus Christ of Latter-day Saints, or the Mormon Church] faith, she says, "I think it's wonderful that women get to stay home and raise their children. Polygamy was a good thing while it lasted and did what it was designed to do. Today we have the fastest-growing American religion on the planet."

Mormonism: Big on Historically Traditional Family Values

Though Emma Smith fervently denied it and most Mormons won't talk about it, even [founder] Joseph Smith was a highly successful polygamist. In the award-winning book *In Sacred Loneliness: The Plural Wives of Joseph Smith*, scholar and historian Dr. Todd Compton meticulously documents how the founder of the Latter-day Saint religion had in fact as many as 33 wives, though most of these marriages were kept secret from the public. In fact, Compton's book chronicles how Joseph's covert second marriage to 16-year-old neighbor Fanny

Mormon Women's Defenses for Polygamy

If Mormon women used communalistic reasoning to construct suffrage rights, they saved their most distinctive and creative arguments about women's authority to defend polygamy. They claimed that polygamy did not subjugate women to men's whims; on the contrary, it gave plural wives freedom and opportunities monogamous women could never experience. Polygamy, they argued, helped relieve loneliness, provided opportunities for intimate female friendship, made sharing household and child-care responsibilities possible, and emancipated wives from many marital duties. Some even maintained that polygamy meant that women need not live for men, nor men for women (though this latter belief was not dominant).

Ethan R. Yorgason,
Transformation of the Mormon Culture Region.
Urbana: University of Illinois Press, 2003.

Alger was so secret that his first wife Emma did not know about [it] until she saw them together and threw her out [of] the house. Joseph's sudden and secret polygamy, though well within biblical precedent, contributed to Emma's infamous apostasy later in life.

Is this news to you? Dr. Compton is an active and respected member of the LDS faith. Consider the monogamy of Joseph Smith a myth that has been totally busted by Mormons and Gentiles [a non-Mormon] alike.

Utah's most famous polygamous practitioner, of course, was an unusually maritally prolific icon of local history: Brigham Young.

While Latter-day Saints tend to pride themselves with their genealogical record keeping, Young's wives had trouble staying on the records for some strange reason. Modern scholars indicate the tally is now at 55. Contrary to the bizarre myth that polygamy was reserved for widows, only 21 of Young's wives had never married before; 6 even had living spouses. Most of the marriages were indeed consummated, and about one-half of the brides were around half his age or less at the time of the marriage.

Considering the ubiquitous nature of polygamy through history and the clear documentation of its practice by revered religious leaders, it seems odd that modern Christians, especially Mormons, are so shy about their history and frequently cover it up with a clearly mythological monogamistic mindset. Besides, political maneuvering aside, mainstream Mormonism *still* preaches that polygamy will be practiced in heaven, so the faithful had better start warming back up to it!

Even [author] Mark Twain, who said he wanted to see the LDS church "extirpated" and called the Book of Mormon "chloroform in print," felt a sense of awe and wonder when he traveled to Utah in the 1870s and met a polygamist family firsthand. He described the encounter in his autobiography, *Roughing It*:

> Our stay in Salt Lake City amounted to only two days, and therefore we had no time to make the customary inquisition into the workings of polygamy and get up the usual statistics and deductions preparatory to calling the attention of the nation at large once more to the matter. I had the will to do it. With the gushing self-sufficiency of youth I was feverish to plunge in headlong and achieve a great reform here— until I saw the Mormon women. Then I was touched. My heart was wiser than my head. It warmed toward these poor, ungainly and pathetically "homely" creatures, and as I turned to hide the generous moisture in my eyes, I said, "No—the man that marries one of them has done an act of Christian charity which entitles him to the kindly applause of man-

kind, not their harsh censure—and the man that marries sixty of them has done a deed of open-handed generosity so sublime that the nations should stand uncovered in his presence and worship in silence."

With compelling arguments like these, religion and scripture on your side, ladies, how could one possibly say no?

Periodical and Internet Sources Bibliography

The following articles have been selected to supplement the diverse views presented in this chapter.

Nigel Barber	"The Wide World of Polygamy: We Hate It, Others Love It," *Psychology Today*, April 19, 2009.
Economist	"Cults of Violence: How Student Fraternities Turned into Powerful and Well-Armed Gangs," July 31, 2008.
Rebecca Evans and Paul Bracchi	"The Satanists of Ash Tree Close: 'Evil' Paedophile Found Guilty of Running Sex Cult from Cul-De-Sac in Seaside Village," *Daily Mail*, March 10, 2011.
Mary Jo Fay	"Polygamist Cults Aren't the Only Source of Abuse and Manipulation," *Denver Post*, May 14, 2008.
Bill Hewitt and Bob Meadows	"Raided! Inside the Polygamy Sect," *People*, April 21, 2008.
Jun Hongo	"Last Trial Brings Dark Aum Era to End," *Japan Times*, November 22, 2011.
Marianne Mott	"Ritual Cat Sacrifices a Halloween Myth, Experts Say," *National Geographic News*, October 26, 2007.
Dorothy Allred Solomon	"The Cult That Wants My Kids," *Marie Claire*, April 14, 2008.
David Von Drehle	"The Texas Polygamist Sect: Uncoupled and Unchartered," *Time*, April 24, 2008.
Heike Zafar	"Difficult to Escape, Abusive Satanic Cults Exist in the Shadows of Society," Deutsche Welle, August 13, 2010. www.dw.de.

OPPOSING
VIEWPOINTS®
SERIES

CHAPTER 3

Why Do People Join Cults?

Chapter Preface

According to some experts, cults actively recruit members at colleges and universities. "They look for intelligent, idealistic, spiritually curious young people who will have good earning potential, and students meet their criteria in every way," says Ian Haworth, founder of the Cult Information Centre in the United Kingdom. "Add to that the fact that they will be disorientated, in a totally new environment with nothing familiar around them," he continues, "and they are a perfect target for these groups."

Haworth advises that campuses must increase awareness of cults and their dangers, as many cults misrepresent themselves as benign or legitimate, until it is "too late" and recruitments of students have taken place. "They will meet criteria for a booth on campus, but it can be a gateway," maintains Doni Whitsett, a clinical professor at the University of Southern California's School of Social Work. "There's no control over what happens off campus." She explains that cults use invitations to dinners, retreats, and lectures to attract students.

In Washington, DC, a student at Howard University, who chooses to remain anonymous, believes her close friend and fellow classmate was recruited by the International Churches of Christ (ICOC) at school. "They approached him in a friendly way, and I supported him at first, because he wanted to get closer to God," she states. "He is one of my best friends, so to see him go from being really enthusiastic and outgoing to withdrawn and unresponsive really bothered myself and his family." However, the ICOC rebukes allegations that the organization is a cult. "I think that absolutely we don't define ourselves as a cult. Basically, people label something a cult, religious or otherwise, when it's something they don't understand or agree with," says Al Baird, a spokesman and elder at ICOC. Also, in a 2010 poll conducted by *U. Magazine*, 77 percent of students who had been a member of a cult reported that they were not pressured to join, and 73 percent claimed that the groups did not use "mind games" to control them. In the following chapter, the authors attempt to explain why people join cults and the methods used to recruit new members.

> "We do ourselves no favor by continuing to deny the existence of brainwashing or to insist that it is only a tool of our ideological enemies."

Cults Brainwash Their Members

Michael Haag

In the following viewpoint, Michael Haag argues that cults may use forms of brainwashing to force people to perform horrific acts or overpower instincts of self-preservation. He maintains that in "robot theory," individuals can be programmed to kill, and in "Stockholm syndrome," victims can form strong loyalties and identification with harmful leaders. The author opposes the claim that certain weaknesses and personality traits predispose some people to join cults and insists that accepting the existence of brainwashing can protect society against it. Based in the San Francisco Bay area, Haag is a social psychologist and contributor to the Jonestown Report.

As you read, consider the following questions:

1. What is the appeal of brainwashing theory, as stated by the author?

Michael Haag, "Does Brainwashing Exist?," *Jonestown Report*, vol. 10, January 25, 2009. Reproduced by permission of the author.

2. How does the author respond to the fact that the courts reject brainwashing as a criminal defense?

3. In Haag's opinion, what view of ourselves is a myth?

In the last half century, "brainwashing" has taken up residence in the English language, seemingly never to be evicted. And yet we are unable to agree on what constitutes brainwashing or even that it exists. The American Psychological Association, for example, has declined to take a position on brainwashing as a valid psychological concept. The courts have debated whether brainwashing is an acceptable legal defense or not—mostly it's not—and scholars have argued both sides of the issue with no resolution.

But brainwashing is not going away. It seems to be with us and to come into sharp focus every time the media unveils another Patty Hearst, Elizabeth Smart [kidnapping victims who spent long periods of time with their captors], or another Jonestown [in Guyana where more than 900 members of Jim Jones's Peoples Temple died of cyanide poisoning in 1978].

Jonestown especially seems to have captured the popular imagination. Even after 30 years, many Americans know what you are talking about when you mention Jonestown. How could Jonestown happen? How could over 900 people be persuaded to commit suicide? Were they brainwashed?

To some extent, the brainwashing explanation is useful because it gets us off the hook. We're not responsible. It wasn't our fault. "The devil made me do it." Does that mean brainwashing is merely a convenient rationalization to avoid personal responsibility? In 1649, [philosopher] René Descartes argued that "the will is by its nature so free that it can never be constrained." Since then much has changed, and Descartes's assertion has been brought into serious question. There seem to be situations, such as Jonestown, where free will can indeed be constrained.

The tragedy of Jonestown, and what happened that day in November 1978, is well documented, and does not need to be recounted here. But it remains difficult for most people to get their minds around the idea that so many people could be persuaded to kill themselves simply because Jim Jones commanded them to do so. The appeal of the brainwashing theory is that it bridges the gap between common sense (that rational individuals would have refused to comply) and what actually happened (almost everyone drank the poison and died).

Robot Theory

Brainwashing in its most controversial form is sometimes called "robot theory." The idea is that people can be made into robots, such that they will perform the most horrendous acts or behave in ways completely at variance with their prior beliefs and values. This form of brainwashing was popularized in the 1959 book and 1962 movie *The Manchurian Candidate*, in which an American soldier in Korea is programmed by his Communist captors to commit murder on command. Perhaps the Jonestown analog of the Manchurian Candidate is the case of Larry Layton who posed as a defector and accompanied the congressional investigating party to the Port Kaituma airstrip, where five people—including Representative Leo Ryan—were killed, and a dozen more were wounded, including two by Layton. Was Layton acting as a robot, robbed of his free will and programmed by Jim Jones to commit murder? Or was he fully aware and in control of his actions and therefore responsible for what he had done? The courts found him guilty and he served his time in prison. However, I wonder if even Larry knows what happened to cause him to fire his weapon.

Not every example of brainwashing needs to be as dramatic as robot theory. An example of what might be termed "brainwashing lite" is the "Stockholm syndrome." It refers to the ability of powerful captors, in this case hostage takers, to create in their victims a loyalty and identification that defies reason. The term originated in 1973 during a bank robbery in Stockholm, Sweden, during which the robbers held bank employees hostage for several days. The victims became emotionally attached to the robbers. They actually resisted attempts to rescue them and even defended the robbers after they were freed. Since then other examples of Stockholm syndrome have been reported by the media. After her kidnapping, for example, Patty Hearst joined her captors in the Symbionese Liberation Army [SLA], repudiated her family, and helped the SLA to rob a bank. Also noteworthy are cases of domestic abuse, where it is common for victims to identify with their abusers. They may refuse to leave the abusive relationship and are repeatedly abused as a result. These are examples of brainwashing as well. They demonstrate the potential of those with life-threatening power over us to affect our beliefs and our behavior in ways we ordinarily would have thought impossible.

Some authors have argued that brainwashing theory (robot theory) is unscientific and therefore unproven. That may be so, but it should be pointed out that doing prospective studies to test a theory of brainwashing would be unethical and thus impossible to perform. We cannot subject human subjects to the conditions experienced in Jonestown and in other cults to see if people can be brainwashed or not.

Overcoming Individual Free Will

The courts seem to have firmly rejected brainwashing as a criminal defense, but this does not necessarily mean that brainwashing is a myth. Margaret Singer, a psychologist who interviewed many cult members, including survivors of Jonestown, believed that cults successfully employed brainwashing to overcome the individual's ability to exercise free will. In his 1961 book *Thought Reform and the Psychology of Totalism*, Robert Jay Lifton reports the results of his study of brainwashing (or thought reform as he prefers to call it) in Communist China. He describes eight psychological themes characteristic of thought reform in totalitarian states and cites several case studies of individuals who were subjected to thought reform in China. Lifton and others have made a persuasive case that thought reform exists. But whether it is employed by cults (or new religious movements) such as Peoples Temple, and whether it explains what happened in Jonestown, is another matter. Recently, Lifton has refined his theory and distinguished "world-destroying cults" such as Aum Shinrikyo from others, and he has postulated the characteristics that define them.

More recently 9/11 [referring to the September 11, 2001, terrorist attacks on the United States] and the wars in Iraq and Afghanistan have given us examples of individuals persuaded by powerful leaders and ideology to overcome the normal impulse for self-preservation and society's prohibition against the killing of innocents. The 9/11 attackers knew they would not survive, but they nevertheless trained for months and carried out their attacks, seemingly without hesitation. Their religion, Islam, does not condone the killing of innocent victims such as the office workers and others in the World Trade Center that died. The attackers knew they were not killing combatants but rather innocent people who had never raised a hand against them or their country. While we may never know the specifics of their experiences leading up to the attack, it seems reasonable to conclude that they were strongly influenced by al Qaeda ideology and by a powerful leader, Osama bin Laden.

Since the onset of the wars in Iraq and Afghanistan, many others in these countries have followed in the footsteps of the 9/11 attackers and have become suicide bombers. Most of those killed have been ordinary Iraqi and Afghan civilians, often including women and children. As more and more suicide bombers die in these attacks, al Qaeda has boasted that they have no shortage of people to fill their ranks. As for the rest of us, though, we believe that we could never be brainwashed to become suicide bombers, just as we believe we could never have been persuaded to drink the Kool-Aid in Jonestown.

Blaming the Victim

The suggestion of a few researchers that individual personality factors predispose some people to join cults, bears closer examination. This is an interesting theory to consider, but it is also dangerously close to "blaming the victim." It would be comforting to believe that the people who joined Peoples Temple were those who were highly suggestible, who were emotionally dependent, or who had experienced emotional problems early in life. To hold such a belief, it should be pointed out, is self-protective. One can be reassured by this idea that he or she, being of sterner stuff, would not have joined such a cult.

Many people have trouble accepting that they might be influenced by cults, or they assert that only "weak-minded" people can be brainwashed. In 1961, Stanley Milgram, a social psychologist, conducted a study in which the experimenter ordered ordinary college students to administer what they believed were painful electric shocks to other students in a separate room. As the shocks were increased in intensity, the victims' cries of pain and agony could be heard through the wall. Most of the students were compliant and continued to increase the shocks as the experimenter ordered them to do. The recipients of the shocks were actually confederates of the experimenter and no shocks were actually given. Nevertheless, Milgram's study demonstrated that ordinary people are susceptible, and they will override their own beliefs of what is moral or acceptable behavior if ordered to do so by a powerful person. As Milgram put it in his 1974 book *Obedience to Authority: An Experimental View*:

> Ordinary people, simply doing their jobs, and without any particular hostility on their part, can become agents in a ter-

An Exception to the Rule?

Within family sociology, it used to be the tendency to say of battered wives, "Why don't they just leave the abusive situation? Nobody is holding them there by force." Now it is much better understood that chronic battering can wear down not only the body but also the capacity to make independent decisions about leaving. I fail to see any significant differences between this phenomenon and the phenomenon of the charismatically abused participant in a cult movement. Furthermore, there is no known human behavior (from murder, to suicide, to child abuse, to self-mutilation) that can be experimentally induced in human subjects by force that cannot also be produced by manipulation of the psychological and social environment. Why should brainwashing be the only phenomenon that is an exception to this rule?

Benjamin D. Zablocki, "Exit Cost Analysis:
A New Approach to the Scientific Study of Brainwashing,"
Nova Religio: The Journal of Alternative
and Emergent Religions, vol. 1, no. 2, April 1998.

rible destructive process. Moreover, even when the destructive effects of their work become patently clear, and they are asked to carry out actions incompatible with fundamental standards of morality, relatively few people have the resources needed to resist authority.

Our view of ourselves is often that we are stronger than others, and any attempt to influence our beliefs or change our values will certainly fail. This is a myth. But we continue to believe in our own superiority and immunity to brainwashing despite all of the evidence to the contrary.

Used for Good Purposes?

So far I have discussed brainwashing as a threat to individual freedom and the means of causing ordinary people to commit murder and suicide. But is brainwashing in all its forms only a tool of those wishing to perpetrate evil and injustice, or can it be used for good purposes as well? Our view of brainwashing may be biased and a consequence of our Western culture with its emphasis on individual rights and personal freedom. Unlike the West, Eastern societies do not always put the emphasis on individual interests before collective ones. Certainly the Chinese Communists, with whom the term "washing the brain" originated, viewed it as a positive good. Even today, "re-education" is used in China to rehabilitate those who have fallen into wrong ideas. We Westerners may view this practice as an attack on individual freedom, but from a communal perspective, rehabilitating individuals who have strayed from the flock is the right thing to do.

Even in the West, the exercise of free will and freedom of expression do not always trump the needs of the community. For example, consider our own departments of corrections and rehabilitation. Their job is to reform prison inmates and to instill in them the moral and ethical values we as a society deem necessary. We applaud when a convicted criminal who has been "rehabilitated" is released from prison, publicly apologizes for his past crime, testifies to his redemption, and promises to be a good and law-abiding citizen in the future. Is this so different from what the Chinese are doing in their society?

When our community is perceived to be under threat, individual freedom may be curtailed on a broad scale, and managing or changing public attitudes and beliefs may be employed as an aid in protecting the community. For example, during World War II, American propaganda portrayed the Japanese enemy as subhuman, evil and alien. Extolling the virtues of Japanese culture and art were not popular following the attack on Pearl Harbor. Much effort went into "educating" the American population about the evils of Japan and its people. As a result, few complained when Japanese Americans were forcibly relocated to internment camps. After the war was won, the camps closed and their occupants reintegrated into the general population. America gradually accepted the Japanese again. Japan itself and the Japanese government were rehabilitated in the eyes of Americans, and Japan became a full partner with America and its allies in the post-war world.

What we call brainwashing may depend on what we already accept as desirable ideology. We don't call it brainwashing when mainline churches convert people to widely held religious beliefs. But when new religious movements persuade their adherents to believe in radical ideas, or ideas we perceive as dangerous to us and to our way of life, we are tempted to label them as cults and to perceive their methods as brainwashing.

Accepting the Existence of Brainwashing

To argue that brainwashing does not exist or is unproven flies in the face of what happened in Jonestown. To suggest that the people who died there were of weak or defective personality may simply give us false reassurance that we could never be taken in by a Jim Jones.

We need to accept that in the world today there exist powerful methods of influencing ordinary people, including ourselves, that can change long-held belief systems and behavior. These methods can be used for good or evil. Understanding the power of brainwashing can arm us against it. Developing the technology of brainwashing for the good of our community, however we define that good, can lead to a better world. We do ourselves no favor by continuing to deny the existence of brainwashing or to insist that it is only a tool of our ideological enemies.

"*Cult methods of recruiting, indoctrinating and influencing their members are not exotic forms of mind control, but only more intensely applied mundane tactics of social influence practiced daily by all compliance professionals and societal agents of influence.*"

Cults Do Not Brainwash Their Members

Bruce A. Robinson

In the following viewpoint, Bruce A. Robinson contends that the existence of brainwashing is neither supported by psychology nor employed by cults or new religious movements (NRMs). Perceiving NRMs as threats, the author states, the anticult movement associates these groups with brainwashing to entrap members. Nonetheless, most mental health professionals and associations agree that psychological means cannot produce mind control, and that individuals join NRMs for emotional support and answers to worldly problems—and leave them of their own free will, he declares. The author is the founder of Ontario Consultants on Religious Tolerance, an advocacy group based in Canada.

As you read, consider the following questions:

1. Why has the credibility of the anticult movement dropped, as told by the author?

2. In the author's view, why do some parents of children who have joined NRMs find comfort in the theory of brainwashing?

3. What evidence is cited in the viewpoint to support the nonexistence of mind control in NRM recruitment programs?

During the 1980s and early 1990s, groups in the anticult movement (ACM) promoted the belief that cults were engaged in advanced forms of psychological manipulation of their members. Their techniques were called brainwashing, thought reform, coercive persuasion, totalism, and mind control. ACM groups taught that cults were entrapping their members so that they could not escape, and reducing them to near zombielike status.

The following essay was originally written in 1997 when:

• Anticult movement (ACM) groups were particularly active,

• Some groups forcibly kidnapped members of NRMs [new religious movements] and attempted to deprogram them, and

• Charges of brainwashing were very common. This is the reduction of the members to a near-zombie state through psychological manipulation.

Since then, the credibility of the ACM has dropped precipitously for various reasons:

• Some ACM groups were involved in criminal acts committed during attempts to deprogram people who were in NRMs.

- The public has largely concluded that brainwashing is a hoax.

- Professional religious and mental health associations have issued statements denying the reality of brainwashing by NRMs.

We will use the term *"NRM"* (new religious movement) in place of *"cult"* in this [viewpoint], because of the high negative emotional content and multiplicity of definitions of the latter term.

Beliefs Promoted by the Anticult Movement

Many individuals in the anticult movement (ACM) have attempted to raise public consciousness about what they perceive to be a major public threat, mainly to youth and young adults. They believe that many NRMs are profoundly evil. These groups, which they call "cults" are seen as:

- Recruiting large numbers of young people into their religious groups, by using deceptive techniques.

- Subjecting them to severe mind-control processes that were first developed in Communist countries, and subsequently developed by NRMs to a much higher level of refinement.

- Destroying their followers' ability to think critically and to make independent decisions.

- Endangering their followers. Many groups have induced their members to commit suicide.

Many in the ACM see NRMs as being particularly efficient in attracting normal, intelligent older teens and young adults, and convincing them to:

- Donate major amounts of time and effort to the group,

- Uncritically accept its teachings,

- Conform to their behavioral restrictions and

- Make a permanent commitment to remain in the NRM.

Extensive confirmation for these beliefs has come from disillusioned former NRM members. A small minority of those psychologists who specialize in the mind-control field also support the ACM's conclusions.

ACM beliefs have been widely accepted by the general public and the media. Some small surveys of public opinion in the mid-1990s found that:

- Among a sample of 383 adults from a western U.S. state, 78% said that they believed that brainwashing exists. 38% agreed that *"brainwashing is required to make someone join a religious cult."*

- Among a sample of 1,000 residents of New York State taken before a high-profile tax evasion case involving Reverend [Sun Myung] Moon and the Unification Church, 43% agreed that *"brainwashing is required to make someone change from organized religion to a cult."*

- Among a random sample of Oregonians who had been exposed to media reports on the Rajneesh group [followers of Indian spiritual leader Bhagwan Shree Rajneesh], 69% agreed that members of that group had been brainwashed.

ACM beliefs mesh well with the mind-control themes seen in *The Manchurian Candidate* (1962; remake 2004) and similar horror movies. Many people uncritically accepted these works of imaginative fiction as representing reality. The public has also absorbed misinformation about the efficiency of brainwashing techniques used by the Communists during the Korean War, and allegedly used subsequently by the CIA [US Central Intelligence Agency]. [Sociologist] James T. Richardson comments:

"These techniques included physical coercion and, taken together, can be labeled 'first generation' brainwashing. Now
these techniques are being used, it is claimed, against young
people in Western countries by unscrupulous cult leaders. . . .
When questioned about the obvious logical problem of applying these theories to situations lacking physical coercion,
proponents have a ready, if problematic, answer. They say
that physical coercion has been replaced by 'psychological
coercion,' which they claim is actually more effective than
simple physical coercion. According to brainwashing proponents, this 'second generation' brainwashing theory incorpo-
rates new insights about manipulation of individuals. . . .
The assumption is that it is not necessary to coerce recruits
physically if they can be manipulated by affection, guilt, or
other psychological influences. Simple group pressures and
emotion-laden tactics are revealed as more effective than the
tactics used in the physically coercive Russian, Chinese, and
Korean POW [prisoner of war] situations."

ACM beliefs are also reinforced [by] some feminists, conservative Christians and others who still believe in the widespread existence of satanic ritual abuse (SRA). SRA promoters
claim that secret, underground satanic cults exist on a local,
state, national and international level. The anti-SRA movement teaches that satanists ritually kill tens of thousands of
infants every year in the U.S. Other infants and children are
believed to be programmed to respond as robots without any
degree of self-will. [These] victims can allegedly be triggered
at a later date by sounds, words, images, colors, etc., to mind-
lessly perform prearranged acts in support of the satanic cult.
By the mid-1990s, investigators had not been able to uncover
hard evidence proving the existence of SRA even after a de-
cade and a half of study. By the end of the century, belief in
SRA had largely collapsed, and continues to decline.

Some parents of adult children who have joined NRMs
take comfort in ACM theories because they absolve the par-

"Brainwash," cartoon by Tony Zuvela, www.CartoonStock.com.

ents from any feelings of personal guilt. They can blame the NRM and its leaders for engaging in criminal acts and capturing their children.

With the decline in belief about mind control by NRMs, ACM groups have largely abandoned their deprogramming in favor of exit counseling programs.

Beliefs Promoted by Other Groups

Mental health professionals and academics who study religions have formed a near consensus that this type of mind control cannot be achieved by psychological means. They observe people entering NRMs because of the emotional support and certainty of belief that the religious groups supply. Almost all later leave the group of their own volition, when their continued membership is no longer a positive experience. The average length of membership is probably less than two years. Some statements by mental health and religious communities follow:

The Society for the Scientific Study of Religion

Ronald Enroth of the *Christian Research Institute Journal* wrote in 1994 about a court case involving the Unification Church (*Molko v. Holy Spirit Association [for the Unification of World Christianity]*). It involved allegations of "coercive persuasion" or "brainwashing" in connection with the denomination's conversion practices. He wrote:

> "The Society for the Scientific Study of Religion and the American Sociological Association became signatories in 1989 to the amicus curiae [friend of the court] brief that was put before the U.S. Supreme Court when the *Molko* case advanced to that judicial level. The brief concluded that allegations of 'brainwashing' constitute a 'devastating infringement' of the petitioner's religious practices and threaten 'the integrity of scientific research.'"

In 1990, after having received many requests to evaluate the practicality of brainwashing by religious groups, the society passed a resolution:

> "This association considers that there is insufficient research to permit informed, responsible scholars to reach consensus on the nature and effects of nonphysical coercion and control. It further asserts that one should not automatically equate the techniques involved in the process of physical coercion and control with those of nonphysical coercion and control. In addition to critical review of existing knowledge, further appropriately designed research is necessary to enable scholarly consensus about this issue."

The American Psychological Association (APA)

Philip G. Zimbardo, PhD, wrote an article during 1990 for the *APA Monitor [on Psychology]* titled: "What messages are behind today's cults?" He is professor of psychology at Stanford University and a former APA president. Some excerpts from his article are:

- *"Cult methods of recruiting, indoctrinating and influencing their members are not exotic forms of mind control, but only more intensely applied mundane tactics of social influence practiced daily by all compliance professionals and societal agents of influence."*

- *". . . cult leaders offer simple solutions to the increasingly complex world problems we all face daily. They offer the simple path to happiness, to success, to salvation by following their simple rules, simple group regimentation and simple total lifestyle. Ultimately, each new member contributes to the power of the leader by trading his or her freedom for the illusion of security and reflected glory that group membership holds out."*

- *"Cult mind control is not different in kind from these everyday varieties, but in its greater intensity, persistence, duration, and scope."*

[Sociologist] Ronald Enroth wrote in 1994:

"The American Psychological Association, along with nearly two dozen individual scholars and behavioral scientists, filed an amicus curiae [friend of the court] brief in 1987 in behalf of the Unification Church in the California Supreme Court. . . . The APA and its co-amici argued that there was little scientific support for 'brainwashing' theory. Both the National Council of Churches and the Christian Legal Society filed briefs in this same case."

Analysis by Answers in Action

Bob and Gretchen Passantino of the conservative Christian group Answers in Action have analyzed the ACM belief systems about NRM brainwashing and have found them lacking in credibility:

- Brainwashing experiments have all been unsuccessful. The CIA [US Central Intelligence Agency] used drugs and electroshock during their investigations into mind control. *"Their experiments were failures; they failed to produce even one potential Manchurian Candidate, and the program was finally abandoned."* The brainwashing attempts by Communist military organizations during the Korean War also failed. They were forced to use torture to supplement their mind-control techniques and were able to obtain success in only a few cases. However, ACM promoters appear to believe that modern forms of mind control within religious organizations represent a major advance over earlier primitive brainwashing techniques. The Passantinos question how relatively uneducated NRM leaders could succeed when highly trained experts had earlier failed.

- They wonder how NRMs can brainwash recruits in a week, while professionals failed after years of indoctrination. They quote the writings of sociologists [David G.] Bromley and [Anson D.] Shupe which point out how absurd this idea is: *". . . the brainwashing notion implied that somehow these diverse and unconnected [religious] movements had simultaneously discovered and implemented highly intrusive behavioral modification techniques. Such serendipity and coordination was implausible given the diverse backgrounds of the groups at issue. Furthermore, the inability of highly trained professionals responsible for implementing a variety of modalities for effecting individual change, ranging from therapy to incarceration, belie claims that such rapid transformation can routinely be accomplished by neophytes against an individual's will."*

- The ACM movement has collected some information to support its belief that religious groups successfully employ mind-control techniques. But the data is unreliable. The information typically represents a very small sample size. It is not practical to obtain information before, during and after an individual has been in an NRM. Often, their data is disproportionately obtained from former members of a religious organization who have been convinced during ACM counseling that they have been victims of mind control.

- One good indicator of the nonexistence of mind-control techniques is the ineffectiveness of NRM recruitment programs. *"Eileen Barker documents that out of 1000 people persuaded by the Moonies [members of the Unification Church founded by Sun Myung Moon] to attend one of their overnight programs in 1979, 90% had no further involvement. Only 8% joined for more than one week. . . ."*

- Another indicator of the nonexistence of mind control is the high turnover rate of members. Eileen Barker mentions that there is a 50% attrition rate during the members' first two years.

- The opinions of former NRM members who have left on their own are clear. Barker comments: *". . . those who leave voluntarily are extremely unlikely to believe that they were ever the victims of mind control."*

The Passantinos conclude: *". . . the Bogey Man of cult mind control is nothing but a ghost story, good for inducing an adrenaline high and maintaining a crusade, but irrelevant to reality."*

Analysis by the Institute for the Study of American Religion

J. Gordon Melton is the author of the three-volume set *"Encyclopedia of American Religions."* He directs the Institute for the Study of American Religion. The Cult Awareness Network quotes him as saying:

> "Slowly, the collapse of the brainwashing hypothesis in relation to the new religions is being brought to Europe, though as in America it will be some years before the strong prejudice against the new religions which has permeated Western culture will be dissolved."

Analysis by the Association for World Academics for Religious Education [AWARE]

The new Cult Awareness Network quotes AWARE as stating:

> "Because of its vested interest in maintaining the conflict, the anticult movement has been unresponsive to objective scholarly studies, and has proceeded with business as usual, as if these studies were nonexistent. Scholars whose work directly challenges the 'cult' stereotype are dismissed as either naive or as being in collusion with the cults. Rather than responding directly to mainstream social science, a small band of anti-cultists with academic credentials have instead conducted research on their own terms, and have created alternative periodicals which featured studies supporting the worst accusations against NRMS."

> " . . . Without the legitimating umbrella of brainwashing ideology, deprogramming—the practice of kidnapping members of NRMs and destroying their religious faith—cannot be justified, either legally or morally. While advocates claim that deprogramming does nothing more than reawaken cult members' capacity for rational thought, an actual examination of the process reveals that deprogramming is little more than a heavy-handed assault on deprogrammers' belief systems. The vast majority of deprogrammers have little or no

background in psychological counseling. They are, rather, 'hired gun' vigilantes whose only qualifications, more often than not, are that they are physically large or that they are themselves ex-cult members."

Analysis by James T. Richardson

Dr. Richardson is a professor of sociology and judicial studies, University of Nevada, Reno. He has written extensively on NRMs and brainwashing. In the mid-1990s, he claimed that:

- Modern brainwashing theories misrepresent earlier academic work on coercive processes developed in Russia, China and Korea. Those techniques were "*generally rather ineffective.*"

More recent studies have shown that:

- NRMs seem to have a generally positive impact on most of their followers.

- Many participants actually seek out the NRMs "*in order to learn about them and experiment with different lifestyles.*"

If the NRMs had access to powerful brainwashing techniques, one would expect that:

- NRMs would have high growth rates. In fact, most have not had notable success in recruitment.

- NRMs would be more successful in retaining members. In fact, most adherents participate for only a short time.

He said that many legal cases have been based on brainwashing theories, and have often been successful.

- "Thus, the past two or three decades have seen the development of a very powerful 'social weapon' to use against unpopular groups (both political and religious) within America."

He said:

- "Brainwashing claims . . . have been used to justify in part some quite dramatic actions (or inactions) by authorities around the world. It may be months or years before the authorities find out that they cannot substantiate such claims and the situation is rectified. Meanwhile, adults may spend months in prison, . . . have their children retained by authorities for some time, or be placed in a mental institution for 'deprogramming' against their will."

| "The cult experience can exert a significant force on the personality and can be better understood by reviewing how a normal personality develops."

Psychological Traits Can Influence People to Join Cults

Frank MacHovec

Frank MacHovec is an adjunct instructor in psychology at Lake-Sumter Community College in Leesburg, Florida, and author of Cults and Terrorism. *In the following viewpoint excerpted from* Cults and Terrorism, *MacHovec states that psychological traits can help determine susceptibility to cults. Applying the five-factor model of personality theory, he claims that extroversion, agreeableness, conscientiousness, openness, and emotional instability can predispose a person to join a cult. Nonetheless, MacHovec contends, relying solely on psychological traits—which only describe behaviors—to determine why people join cults is simplistic.*

As you read, consider the following questions:

1. What does the author say about the stability and strength of traits?

Frank MacHovec, *Cults and Terrorism*, Lulu.com, 2011. Reproduced by permission of the author.

2. How does MacHovec describe the trait of agreeableness?

3. How can conscientiousness increase susceptibility to cults, in MacHovec's view?

Normal psychological development involves concepts that can also be applied to a cult experience. A person's normal baseline behavior is her or his *pre-cult* mind. The cult experience can exert a significant force on the personality and can be better understood by reviewing how a normal personality develops.

Personality: The Five Major Theories

TYPES AND TRAITS

Types or typologies and traits are the oldest personality theories. Empedocles, a student of [Greek mathematician and philosopher] Pythagoras in the 5th century BCE described personality as types of character and temperament. By the 3rd century BCE [Greek physician] Hippocrates taught four types: sanguine (blood-based as in "red-blooded" active people), melancholic (moody or depressed from black bile), choleric, (antagonistic or irritable from high yellow bile), or phlegmatic (calm or lethargic from too much phlegm). In recent times this theory was further refined by psychologist Hans Eysenck into three traits: extraversion-introversion, neuroticism, and psychoticism. Psychiatrist Carl Jung described three traits on continua: extraversion-introversion, sensing-intuiting, and thinking-feeling. [Psychologist] Isabel Briggs Myers added a 4th continuum: judgment-perception. Psychologist Gordon Allport defined a trait as "a neuropsychic structure having the capacity to render many stimuli functionally equivalent and to initiate and guide equivalent meaningful consistent forms of adaptive and expressive behavior" (1961).

Personality types are generalized classifications of personality. Another example of personality types theory is the *Type A* and *Type B* personalities that were popular 50 years ago.

Type A are strong-willed, driven people supposedly at high risk of heart disease because of continued high stress. *Type B* are less driven more laid back, supposedly at lower risk of stress-induced health problems. Research has shown that some *Type A* people do not develop heart disease, and some *Type B* people do. Hostility (a trait) correlates more to heart disease risk. The research data exposes the danger of oversimplification and overgeneralization.

Traits can be parts of a type but not global enough to be types. For example, an extrovert can be open, agreeable, and conscientious, basic traits in 5-factor theory. Extroversion and introversion are the oldest reported personality types. Psychiatrist Carl Jung included them in his types theory and added *sensing vs. intuiting* and *thinking vs. feeling.* Isabel Myers Briggs and her mother Katharine Briggs developed the Myers-Briggs [Type Indicator] instrument to assess those three continua and added *judging vs. perceiving.* [Psychologist] David Keirsey developed a shorter test which is included in his book *Please Understand Me.*

Personality traits, like types, have been observed and reported throughout history in poetry, prose, and drama. The *Diagnostic and Statistical Manual [of Mental Disorders]* of the American Psychiatric Association defines personality traits as "enduring patterns of perceiving, relating to, and thinking about the environment and oneself exhibited in a wide range of social and personal contexts." Traits are relatively stable over time, thus recognizable, and strong enough to influence behavior. Traits are the oldest personality theory, dating back to the ancient Greeks and probably before. In addition to his four personality types, Hippocrates also described traits, such as outgoing (extroverted) and inner-directed (introverted) behaviors.

20th-century psychologists developed an increasingly long list of traits. Gordon Allport classified what he called "dispositions" as *cardinal* if predominant, or *central* when basic to the individual, *secondary* when weaker. Allport and [H.S.] Odbert distilled 18,000 key words used to describe personality into 4500 observable relatively permanent traits. Raymond Cattell used oblique factor analysis to isolate *16 primary factors*, popularly known as "the 16 PF" and five *secondary factors*. Using orthogonal factor analysis, Hans Eysenck simplified the traits into three basics: *extraversion, neuroticism,* and *psychoticism.* Lewis Goldberg proposed a five-factor model of *openness, conscientiousness, extroversion, agreeableness,* and *neuroticism* (later changed to emotional stability) which has psychology's preferred personality theory. The five factors are:

Extroversion. High scorers are actively involved in the external world, enjoy being with people, are enthusiastic, often experience positive emotions. In groups they like to talk. Introverts tend to be quiet, deliberate, less involved in the external world, may not be due to shyness or depressions—they need less stimulation and prefer to be alone more.

Agreeableness supports social harmony and mutual cooperation, in friendly, considerate, helpful, open compromise. Agreeable people are basically trustworthy, but agreeableness is not useful where objective or tough decisions are needed and seemingly disagreeable people can be competent scientists, critics, or soldiers.

Conscientiousness controls and directs impulses not necessarily negative. Sometimes quick action is needed and a first impulse effective. Conscientious people succeed by planning and persisting, regarded positively by others but can be seen as dull and may be perfectionists.

Openness to experience is being creative, curious, more aware of feelings than closed people, usually with unconventional beliefs. It increases with education but correlates weakly to tested IQ and creativity. Closed people tend to be conservative, with narrower interests, and prefer the predictable and familiar over novelty. Openness can be positive for a professor but not in sales and service occupations.

Neuroticism (is now *emotional stability*). Such people are more emotionally reactive and tend to interpret ordinary situations negatively. Their feelings persist so they can often be moody, interfering with decisive thinking and coping with stress. The more stable, the less easily upset, more resilient, but doesn't mean more positive feelings (more extroverted).

A Major Weakness

A major weakness of traits theory is that it is simplistic. It only describes a behavior. It doesn't explain its underlying cause. Relying only on traits is oversimplification, overgeneralization, and lacks the detail needed to fully understand personality or plan effective therapy. Types theory is similar but not identical to traits theory in that both rely on fixed behaviors. The major difference is that types are usually described in terms of opposites (e.g., extroversion and introversion). Neither adequately describes gray areas. For example, most people are ambiverts [have characteristics of both extrovert and introvert]. Pure extroverts or introverts are very rare. Behavioral scientists needed more precision in identifying and assessing discrete categories and their relative strengths. Five-factor theory is psychology's attempt to isolate basic personality dynamics more objectively but is not the long-sought unified personality theory. Many psychologists feel Cattell's 16 PF is as valid.

But types and traits theories have some predictive validity relative to cults. Applying psychology's latest personality theory, the five-factor model, *extroversion*, being comfortable with others, would increase susceptibility, as would *agreeableness* and *openness*. *Conscientiousness* would facilitate commitment to cult life. *Emotional stability* would be a defense but *neuroticism*, its opposite, would likely increase susceptibility.

| "Cults use every available means to gain new members, but why do people join cults? Four basic reasons have been identified."

People Join Cults for a Variety of Reasons

Robin Jackson

Based in Durban, South Africa, Robin Jackson is a former cult member and author of Cults: How They Work. *In the following viewpoint excerpted from* Cults, *Jackson describes four reasons people join cults. First, he points out, those who join for intellectual reasons seek authoritative answers to questions about human life and personal identity. Individuals who join for emotional reasons, Jackson continues, have unfulfilled emotional needs or have suffered a significant loss. People who join for social reasons have a disrupted sense of belonging, ranging from family dysfunction to alienation from politics, he suggests. Finally, Jackson states, the decline of mainstream religion provides spiritual reasons for some to seek cults.*

As you read, consider the following questions:

1. What do some ex-cult members state about their time in a cult, according to Jackson?

Robin Jackson, *Cults: How They Work*, Jacko Consulting, 2008. Reproduced by permission of the author.

2. What example does Jackson provide of when a cult takes advantage of social factors?

3. What happens at the "hyped meeting" of a cult, as explained by Jackson?

People join cults for different reasons. The popularity of so-called "accepted" religions is dwindling quite fast. A recent survey conducted in the United Kingdom reported that many of the mainstream religions have reported rapid decline in membership. This could very well be the trend here in South Africa, and the rest of the Western world. Interest in mysticism, New Age teachings and the occult is certainly growing. More and more people are looking for a spiritual aspect to their lives. If mainstream religion fails to supply this then there are several cults around which appear to promise either guaranteed salvation, or at least a community of like-minded individuals.

There are numerous anticult groups that produce literature warning of the dangers of cult membership. There are also many ex-members who have written accounts about their time in a cult. Some, but not all, would argue that their lives have become more fulfilled by joining a cult. They may also say that their beliefs and way of life are just as valid as anybody else's. However, these groups continue to generate much criticism and to attract publicity (believe me, some court it). This is likely to be adverse when their beliefs are practised in such a way that they not only contradict society's norms, but also are sometimes illegal.

From my experience in a cult and the subsequent research conducted, I, as well as other numerous resources, have noticed a pattern that is used by cults to recruit members. Young people are especially susceptible to cult recruiting techniques and are most often the target. Many cult watch groups such as the UK-based INFORM and the American Cult Awareness

Network tour schools and colleges informing people of the dangers and warning signs as to cult activity.

In 2000 authorities received complaints from families, theologians and ex-members that a controversial international cult was active in recruiting vulnerable youngsters on campuses in Cape Town and up-country. The International Churches of Christ (ICOC) was outlawed from several UK and US universities for its alleged brainwashing and aggressive proselytizing techniques, and for splitting up families. The Rand Afrikaans University banned the group in 1999 after receiving complaints. The University of Pretoria conducted an investigation into the group. Willem Nicol, who was campus priest said: "The ICOC must be exposed. We didn't ban them simply because we did not want to give them publicity. They are a dangerous cult and youngsters need to be protected because they are not allowed to leave once they join."

On its website the ICOC (not to be confused with the mainstream "Church of Christ") boasted of being active at Parow High School, University of Cape Town, University of the Western Cape and [Eastern] Cape Technikon. Cults use every available means to gain new members, but why do people join cults? Four basic reasons have been identified.

Intellectual Reasons

All of us have the ability to be intellectual and to use our reasoning processes. We are forever learning and seeking new ways to enrich our lives. In an unsure world, cults provide authoritative answers to questions that have plagued man for centuries: *Who am I? Why am I here? Where am I going? What does the future hold?* However, this does not mean they provide correct answers. Some provide a false sense of security with answers that play on people's ignorance. Cults prey on this ignorance and try to impress the uninformed with pseudo-scholarship.

The Way International's founder, Victor Paul Wierwille, quoted profusely from Hebrew and Greek to give the impression of scholarship. Jehovah's Witnesses give a similar impression when going from door to door.

Emotional Reasons

Our emotional makeup allows us to experience emotions of joy, love, peace, happiness, kindness and other qualities. However, our emotional makeup also produces qualities of hatred, restlessness, depression, selfishness and so forth. In this way cults appeal to our basic emotional needs. We need a sense of meaningful direction and need to feel loved. Individuals who have emotional problems or have an identity crisis are particularly susceptible to being recruited into a cult. Low points in people's lives, such as the death of a loved one, are the opportunities that cults seek out to employ their recruitment techniques.

Cults take advantage of this and offer ready-made solutions that are ultimately unsatisfying. The cults ultimately tell their followers what to think, how to behave and emphasize dependency on the group or leader for emotional stability.

Social Reasons

People are not solitary beings but social ones. Our relationship to humanity is born from our social influence. We are active in society and fulfill our desire to be part of a group. When group life is disrupted, because of a dysfunctional family, a bad church atmosphere, political issues or burn out at the workplace, people want to drop out of society and the cults are often there to catch them.

The cults also take advantage of other social factors such as when the hypocrisy of some religious leaders comes to the fore. They highlight these incidents and assure their followers that they have made the right move by joining them. However, when the group's own hypocrisy comes to the fore, or their leader's for that matter, these are hurriedly covered up or brushed aside as persecution.

Spiritual Reasons

Many in today's society find themselves spiritually and morally lost. The collapse of religious values has regularly plagued humanity and is not a new phenomenon. That is partly the reason some look to alternative routes to faith and the meaning of existence. Interest in mysticism, New Age teachings and the occult has become very popular in the West where spirituality has been eclipsed by the joys of wealth and material gratification. Some feel that mainstream religion is failing them and therefore they become easy prey for the cults.

Here are the techniques and some key warning signs that could indicate that a cult is trying to recruit you. Of course it may vary from cult to cult as to how these are applied. However, the basis is the same.

Hyped Meetings

Instead of explaining to you up front what the group believes or what their programme is, they will insist that you can only understand it by attending a group meeting. When you go to these meetings everyone around you seems so enthusiastic that you begin to wonder if there is something wrong with you. The environment they create is one where you feel so uncomfortable and the only way to become comfortable is to join in. This is an example of controlled peer pressure. This technique is especially used in commercial cults.

An acquaintance of mine related his experience to me where he was invited to attend one of these meetings. When he arrived everybody in the room was chanting and singing songs in unison. "The atmosphere was overwhelming," he said. Before he knew it he had a bag of books in his hand which he was commissioned to sell from door to door with the promise of great wealth by following their special programme.

Intense and Unrelenting Pressure

They will call on you repeatedly. Frequently they will meet you on campus, at your door or outside your place of work. They will trick you into going to their meetings for an hour but then lead you to a long study, meeting or talk. This intense and unrelenting pressure has to be kept up otherwise you might snap out of the mind-control environment they are trying to immerse you in. One group calls this technique "Return Visits."

They Tell You They Are Not a Cult

Most certainly this is a preemptive strike against the possible warnings you will get from friends and family which they know will come your way. Some cults will even tell you that Satan will send your friends and family to dissuade you from becoming involved with the "one true religion." This tactic often places a warped sense of logic in the new recruit's mind. "The agents of Satan" eventually do come and warn him that it is a cult, so since the group predicted it, the group therefore must be true. Here I must stress, if any group tells you they are not a cult and that some people call them one, then for Pete's sake (and for yours of course) find out why!

Periodical and Internet Sources Bibliography

The following articles have been selected to supplement the diverse views presented in this chapter.

Jack Bragen	"On Mental Illness: Persons with Mental Illness and Cults," *Berkeley Daily Planet*, March 26, 2011.
Ryan Dube	"Why Do People Join Cults?," Reality Uncovered, July 3, 2010. www.realityuncovered.net.
Emily Friedman	"Sect Members: Brainwashed or Believers?," ABC News, April 16, 2008.
Jane Futcher	"Demystifying Cults: Psychiatrist Analyzes Why People Join Groups," *Marin Independent Journal*, July 28, 2010.
Kola Ibrahim and Ayo Ademiluyi	"Nigeria: Mass-Based Student Unionism Could Counterweight Cultism," *Pambazuka News*, July 2, 2009.
Jillian Risberg	"Predators on Campus: An Inside Look at Cults in New Jersey," Newsroom Jersey, December 1, 2009. www.newjerseynewsroom.com.
Luis Santamaria del Rio	"The Internet as a New Place for Sects," *Cultic Studies Review*, vol. 7, no. 1, 2008.
Richard Zwolinski	"6 Reasons I Was an Easy Target for a Cult," *Therapy Soup*, December 15, 2011. http://blogs .psychcentral.com.

CHAPTER 4

How Can Cult Members Be Helped?

Chapter Preface

Exit counseling is an intervention method used to convince a person to leave a cult. Different from deprogramming, the approach does not involve coercive practices or restraint of the cult member. "Exit counseling refers to a voluntary, intensive, time-limited, contractual educational process that emphasizes the respectful sharing of information with cultists," state cult experts Michael D. Langone and the late Paul Martin. Also, the role of the family takes greater importance and involvement. "Although deprogrammers prepare families for the process, exit counselors tend to work more closely with families and expect them to contribute more to the process; that is, exit counseling requires that families establish a reasonable and respectful level of communication with their loved one before the exit counseling . . . can begin," Langone and Martin maintain.

According to cult consultant Joe Szimhart, exit counseling is characterized by the following practices: exit counselors do not usually offer one-on-one services to avoid liability; the cult member can stop the sessions at any given time; the cult member can have the exit counselor leave the premises; and the family may persist in urging the cult member to remain in the intervention. "Due to the education shared during exit counseling, recovery begins during the process," Szimhart says. "Recovery means that 'stop and think' parts of the brain have been re-engaged regarding ingrained beliefs, charismatic attachments, and constricted behaviors," he adds.

Moreover, professionals propose that the aim of exit counseling is to create an intellectual reaction in the cult member rather than one based on emotion. "Very seldom is a visible 'snapping' moment seen—but a gradual increase in interest, interaction, and feedback with the information—often accompanied with an increase of interest in and interaction with the family," suggests Carol Giambalvo, a thought-reform consultant. In the following chapter, the authors investigate and critique how current and former cult members can be helped.

> "*Cult deprogramming [is] 'providing members with information about the cult and showing them how their own decision-making power had been taken away from them.'*"

Ex-Cult Members Can Be Deprogrammed

Rick Alan Ross

In the following viewpoint, Rick Alan Ross proposes that deprogramming can be used to remove individuals from cult involvement. Over the years, Ross explains, deprogramming has been developed and refined to effectively show cult members how thought reform compromises their abilities to think critically and independently. He says that the involvement of family members and friends is vital and serves two objectives: to motivate the cult member to participate voluntarily and to offer the deprogrammer eyewitness accounts of his or her behaviors. Ross is a renowned cult deprogrammer and founder of the Rick A. Ross Institute, which offers a database of articles, court cases, and other materials on cults.

Rick Alan Ross, "Cult Deprogramming: An Examination of the Intervention Process," *Schenzhen International Symposium on Cultic Studies*, 2010. Reproduced by permission of the author.

As you read, consider the following questions:

1. What do professionals involved in cult intervention call their work, as stated by Ross?

2. What is the status of involuntary deprogramming in the United States, as described by Ross?

3. How does Ross describe his success rate?

My work regarding cult deprogramming began in 1982. At that time, I was deeply concerned about a group that had infiltrated a nursing home where my 82-year-old grandmother was a resident. The group had specifically asked its members to seek jobs as paid professional staff at the nursing home, with the ulterior motive of targeting residents for recruitment.

My grandmother made me aware of this situation. And working with the executive director of the nursing home, we identified the group members on staff, who were subsequently terminated. This personal experience initiated me in the world of radical religious groups and cults. I then became an anticult community activist and organizer.

During this period, I was appointed to two national committees and later asked to join the professional staff of a social service agency in Phoenix, Arizona. At the agency, it was not uncommon for parents to bring an adult child, typically a college student, to my office for consultation regarding involvement in a radical group or cult.

I would work with the families often in conjunction with our staff psychologist and/or caseworkers, in an effort to extricate the individual from any further cult involvement. Little did I know at the time that this process of intervention was called "cult deprogramming."

During the 1980s, I was involved in about 100 interventions regarding cultlike groups. Families would find me through the previously mentioned social service agency, a community educational bureau that also employed me or were referred by local clergy, educators and community leaders.

During this period, I worked largely within the Jewish community; though increasingly through related conferences and professional exchanges, I became aware of a network of anticult activists and helping professionals throughout the United States. It was through my interaction with others doing essentially the same work that I later learned the type of intervention work that I was doing was known as cult deprogramming.

Defining Cult Deprogramming

Margaret Singer, often cited as a leading brainwashing and cult expert, defined cult deprogramming as "providing members with information about the cult and showing them how their own decision-making power had been taken away from them."

Over the years, that basic process of snaring information and demonstrating to cult members how the power of persuasion may have compromised their critical and independent thinking has been refined continuously and improved. In fact, the name "cult deprogramming" itself has become something of a politically incorrect term. Today most professionals engaged in cult intervention work prefer other labels to describe their work, for example, "exit counseling," "thought reform consultation," or "strategic intervention therapy." Many believe that cult deprogramming can only be applied correctly to involuntary cult interventions.

However, the simple distilled definition provided by Singer remains the most salient and basic understanding of the process to bring people out of destructive cults through intervention.

Involuntary deprogramming with adults is no longer done within the United States. The only involuntary interventions done regarding cults within North America would be with minor children under the direct supervision of their custodial parent. Legal concerns have precluded anything else, though for a relatively brief time during the 1970s through a court provision known as conservatorship, involuntary deprogramming did occur with adults.

In 1986, I began working privately. That is, my work began as a private consultant and cult intervention specialist. Over the past 24 years, I have been involved in hundreds of intervention efforts. My work has taken me throughout the United States, and to Canada, Italy, Sweden, England, Ireland and Israel.

I have continually developed and refined my intervention approach. The basic foundation as defined by Singer remains the same, but the details of that process have evolved, especially in consideration of the improved technology available and access to information through the Internet.

In the 1980s and early 1990s, information was provided to cult members during interventions through books, videos and direct interaction with former members.

Today the process of providing information has been directly affected by the advent of the Internet, DVDs, streaming video, teleconferencing and other technologies. These advancements have made the gathering and organizing of information for an intervention much easier. The preparation, presentation and communication approach has been honed and refined over the years.

My hope in presenting this [viewpoint] is that I can share with you the basic structure and content of my approach in concise language. By sharing my approach with you, we can hopefully better understand and further the development of cult intervention work.

A True Moment of Enlightenment

In one sense, deprogramming confirms that some drastic change takes place in the workings of the mind in the course of a cult member's experience, for only through deprogramming does it become apparent to everyone, including the cult member, that his actions, expressions and even his physical appearance have not been under his own control. In another sense, deprogramming is itself a form of sudden personality change. Because it appears to be a genuinely broadening, expanding personal change, it would seem to bear closer resemblance to a true moment of enlightenment, to the natural process of personal growth and newfound awareness and understanding, than to the narrowing changes brought about by cult rituals and artificially induced group ordeals.

Flo Conway and Jim Siegelman, Snapping: America's Epidemic of Sudden Personality Change. *New York: Stillpoint Press, 1995.*

Preparation

The first step in the process of any intervention is preparation.

After a family, spouse or someone concerned contacts me requesting an intervention, I must evaluate the situation and assemble a file.

This file includes an intake questionnaire which is composed of about 50 questions, which deal with the individual cult member's background, history of involvement and specific concerns regarding the immediate situation.

Additionally, I will also collect for my file information specifically about the group and/or leader in question.

Most often a series of phone consultations will follow.

Then there will be a sit-down meeting typically the day before the intervention begins.

In this process of preparation, the family identifies who would be most effective for participation at the intervention. That is, which family members have the most respect, admiration and emotional hold on the cult-involved individual? The net result of this preparation process is the specific determination of who will become a member of the intervention team.

After identifying and assembling the team, here is what is usually discussed at the preparation meeting:

- What are the rules of engagement?

- What are the boundaries and parameters of participation?

- What roles will each family member or friend play?

- What should they say or not say?

- How will the intervention process begin, proceed and ultimately end?

The basic role [of] each family member and friend can best be summarized as largely focused upon two primary objectives. These objectives are:

1. Essentially anchor the cult-involved individual; that is, keep them from leaving by helping to create an atmosphere of support premised upon historical trust and understanding. Simply put, the cult member will not stay involved in the intervention process for my sake, as I am a total stranger. But the cult member will stay out of respect for their family, friends and others concerned. This is vitally important because any intervention done with an adult is on a voluntary basis and dependent upon their consent and ongoing cooperation. In the preparation process, possible scenarios or potential situations are discussed. For example, the individual may

become angry, get up and begin to leave. How should that be handled? Who would be most effective in persuading him or her not to leave and to stay?

2. The family and friends working with me also are there to provide firsthand eyewitness testimony. That is, what have they seen and observed regarding recent behavior, which has caused them concern? At various times during an intervention, a cult member may engage in denial. Since I have not directly witnessed what has occurred, I rely upon the family and friends present to share their experience.

We also must discuss and define our roles.

What is the role of the intervention specialist?

When is it appropriate and effective for family and friends to interject their opinions, testimony and concern?

I typically will advise the family to allow me the role of presenting the main body of information, leading and/or facilitating the discussion.

The Intervention

An average cult intervention takes 3 to 4 days, not including travel or preparation.

This means approximately 24 to 32 working hours spread out at eight hours per day.

The more time I have, the more likely it is that the cult member will leave the group.

About 75% of my interventions have ended in success. That is, the individual that was the focus of the intervention decided to leave the cult at its conclusion.

Most of my failures occurred within the first day or 24 hours of the intervention.

Very few cult members I have worked with for 3 to 4 days chose to continue with the group. Ultimately what this means is that the more time that I have, the more likely it is that the intervention will be successful.

An intervention is an ongoing dialog or discussion. During such a discussion, everyone present offers their impressions, observations and opinions. My role is to lead and facilitate that ongoing discussion, often directing and focusing attention on specific points.

There are four basic blocks or areas of discussion essential for the completion of an effective and potentially successful intervention.

These blocks of discussion preferably can be discussed in the order that follows, but this sequence may be rearranged during the intervention, due to the interest and focus of the cult-involved individual.

The four blocks of discussion are:

1. What is the definition of a destructive cult?

2. How does the process of coercive persuasion or thought reform really work?

3. What is the history of the group and/or leader that has drawn concern?

4. What are the family's concerns?

> "Deprogramming seemed to involve ap-
> plying the same techniques that had
> been used to 'brainwash' religious devo-
> tees to 'unbrainwash' them."

Some Cult Deprogrammers
Are as Harmful as Cults

Dominic Streatfeild

*Based in the United Kingdom, Dominic Streatfeild is a journal-
ist, documentarian, and author of* Brainwash: The Secret History of Mind Control. *In the following viewpoint excerpted
from* Brainwash, *Streatfeild contends that some efforts to deprogram, or un-brainwash, cult members have been counterproductive and harmful. Streatfeild believes that early deprogramming
employed similar techniques as brainwashing itself, including
imprisonment, repetition, and physical force. Moreover, as cults
became wary of deprogrammers' kidnappings, the author says,
they became more closed and secretive. While deprogrammers
won a temporary victory in the press, he claims, their practice
was later viewed as stripping young people of their religious beliefs by force.*

Dominic Streatfeild, *Brainwash: The Secret History of Mind Control,* New York: Thomas
Dunne Books, 2007; Hodder & Stoughton, 2007. © 2007 by Dominic Streatfeild. Repro-
duced by permission of Thomas Dunne Books, an imprint of St. Martin's Press and
Hodder & Stoughton Ltd.

As you read, consider the following questions:

1. Why was persuading religious converts to participate in brainwashing proved impossible, as stated by the author?

2. How did cults' efforts to stop kidnappings affect deprogrammers' views of these groups, in Streatfeild's view?

3. What happened in the case of deprogrammer Galen Kelly, as told by the author?

The technique [of deprogramming] had its roots in an incident that took place in San Diego on Independence Day 1971 when Ted Patrick, California governor Ronald Reagan's special representative for community relations, lost his teenage son, Michael, at Mission Beach. When Michael showed up at the family hotel later that night, he told his father that he had been accosted by some young evangelists with guitars. They had told him that if he came home with them he wouldn't have to go to school anymore and that he would never have to do any work. He shouldn't go home, they said, because his parents were evil. The evangelists were so persuasive, Michael said, that he had almost had to drag himself away. They had called themselves the Children of God [a religious organisation also once known as the Family of Love and currently known as the Family International].

Patrick didn't give the matter much thought until, back at work a week later, he was contacted by a woman who claimed she had lost her teenage son at the same beach on the same day: the boy had wandered off, been accosted by the Children of God and never returned. When he began to collect information about the organisation further reports emerged. The stories were identical: a teenager vanished and then, a week or so later, called his parents and told them that they were evil; the Children of God were his family now and he wasn't coming home. Sometimes, in the background, the parents heard their child being told what to say by another group member. After just two days' research, Patrick had allegedly collected near-identical reports from twenty-six separate families.

At the end of July Patrick went undercover on Mission Beach, deliberately getting himself recruited by the Children of God to see what they were up to. He was driven to a hot, crowded house where he was encouraged to hand over his car and various other possessions. Then he was lectured to, prayed over, made to sing religious songs and hectored. Luke 14:26 ('if anyone comes to me and does not hate his own father and mother . . . he cannot be my disciple') was cited and the recruits were told that this proved they should reject their parents in favour of the organisation. Exhausted, Patrick was finally allowed to sleep only at four a.m. on his third night in the compound. Three hours later he was woken up and the process started again. The next day, desperate to escape, he told staff that he was ready to give all his possessions to the group and, under the pretext of going to fetch them, took a taxi home. He was shaken by the experience: another twenty-four hours in the compound, he thought, and he would have been converted himself.

Convinced that something deeply sinister was going on, Patrick and parents like him turned to the brainwashing literature and, in particular, the work of a psychiatrist called Robert Jay Lifton. Lifton, who had served in the US Air Force in the 1950s, was one of a handful of doctors allowed access to prisoners of war returning from Korea. In 1961 he had written a seminal study of the brainwashing phenomenon, *Thought Reform and the Psychology of Totalism*. In chapter 22, he described eight specific techniques that could be used by an ideological group to disorient anyone. Ranging from 'loading the language' (introducing technical jargon that limited, rather than enhanced, the ability to think critically, thus stifling dissent) to 'milieu control' (restricting communications to ensure that doubt and dissent couldn't get in from outside), the eight techniques of 'ideological totalism' seemed to offer potential brainwashers a means of controlling virtually anybody.

Patrick and the other parents concluded that the new religious organisations were using all eight of Lifton's techniques simultaneously, together with food and sleep deprivation and sensory overload to brainwash their recruits. The method, wrote Patrick, was 'the same as the North Koreans used on prisoners of war'. If toughened US soldiers in Korea couldn't fight it in the 1950s, what chance did fresh-faced American teenagers have in the 1970s?

Applying the Same Techniques

Patrick now began his own crusade against the Children of God. He developed a technique called 'deprogramming' to fight them. It involved sitting new religious converts down and telling them a few hard facts about their chosen religion. He would engage in religious debates until, finally, the acolyte would break down and realise that he had been misled.

That was the theory, anyway. In fact, things worked out rather differently. As might have been predicted, persuading religious converts to take part in a deprogramming session proved impossible. Invariably they had to be lured into a room under some pretext, and then forcibly prevented from leaving. When this proved difficult, they were snatched on the street when they were least expecting it—and kidnapped. Patrick persuaded parents that this kind of treatment was necessary since their children were 'beyond reason'. They had, he said, been turned into 'zombies'.

Even when the youths were kidnapped, though, Patrick faced the problem of getting them to listen to what they were being told. Many religious groups taught recruits to combat doubt by focusing their minds on repetitive and meaningless activities as a means of distracting themselves. The result was that Patrick frequently found himself facing glassy-eyed au-

Cartoon by Dan Rosandich. Reproduced by permission.

tomatons who sat cross-legged and rocked backwards and forwards, chanting. How could you get through to people in that state? His solution was to bully them into listening using repetition, forced incarceration and, on occasion, physical force. But this had repercussions. Although Patrick denied it vociferously, deprogramming seemed to involve applying the same

techniques that had been used to 'brainwash' religious devo-
tees to 'unbrainwash' them. It was quite hard to see where the
techniques differed, except in objective.

As Patrick took to kidnapping young people from religious groups, so more and more parents called and asked for
his help. Soon he and the other key deprogrammer of the
early 1970s, Joe Alexander, were dealing with hundreds of
cases a year. Meanwhile, other deprogrammers started to copy
him. But as kidnappings and deprogrammings multiplied, the
religious groups got smarter. The Unification Church, which
saw itself as under attack from bigoted outsiders, put up fences
around the Boonville [California] compound and stationed a
guardhouse at the gate. According to the church, the fences,
the defensive stance towards outsiders and the secrecy surrounding the organisation would not have been necessary if
people hadn't kept busting in, sometimes armed, and snatching their members. Wasn't it allowed to protect itself?

To the deprogrammers, the fact that the groups were now
walling themselves in made them even more suspect: If the
kids who joined were really free, as they purported to be, why
were they locked in? Why weren't their parents allowed to visit
them? What did they have to hide? As the organisations took
more and more precautions to stop kidnappings, the kidnappings became more elaborate and imaginative. The situation
escalated.

A Macabre Sense of the Absurd

Inside the Unification Church, tales began to multiply about
'deprogramming'. There were rumours that the process involved beatings, degradation, torture and sexual abuse. According to various sources, two members of the Tucson Freedom of Thought Foundation had deprogrammed an Old
Catholic priest because his Episcopalian parents objected to
his choice of religion. Ted Patrick, say some reports, had apparently deprogrammed two Greek Orthodox girls because

their parents were upset that they had resisted the traditional Greek custom of living at home until their parents had found them suitable husbands.

Deprogramming even assumed a macabre sense of the absurd. New York deprogrammer Galen Kelly—who was sentenced to seven years in jail in 1993 for staging a kidnapping on a Circle of Friends devotee, and mistakenly snatching the wrong girl off the street—apparently told a story about how a deprogrammer 'snapped' a young girl out of her 'cult mind' and returned her home. 'You'll be glad to know,' crowed the triumphant deprogrammer, 'that your daughter is a Christian again.'

'But,' gasped the parents, 'she used to be *Jewish*.'

It was no surprise that when Unificationists failed to return home, troops were immediately dispatched to find them. Where had they been snatched from? Where were they being held? Had they been taken to their parents' address for the deprogramming? Pickets were sent out to spy on possible locations and try to snatch back the church member before it was too late. When they found the building, they surrounded it and Moonies [Unificationists, or members of the Unification Church founded by Sun Myung Moon] stood at the windows, chanting messages of love and support to their incarcerated brother or sister inside. For the deprogrammers, being in a building surrounded by chanting Moonies was pretty spooky.

Meanwhile, once the press got hold of the fact that young people were being kidnapped from weird religious groups and 'unbrainwashed', deprogramming became a hot story. Both religious groups and deprogrammers played the media for all they were worth. 'I, believe firmly,' Ted Patrick wrote in his autobiography, 'that the Lord helps those who help themselves—and a few little things like karate, mace, and handcuffs come in handy from time to time.' He later boasted, 'I could snatch a kid from Alcatraz [referring to a federal prison] if I had to.'

Ethically Fraught with Problems

After a successful mission, the newly deprogrammed subject was paraded in front of the cameras to prove that they were happy to be free and glad to have been kidnapped. In press conferences, tales were told of military-type extractions and how truth had triumphed in bringing the children back to their families. If the deprogrammings were unsuccessful, meanwhile, the returned believers would tell stories of horrific abuse and how truth had triumphed in bringing them back to their true family.

Initially, there was so much antipathy regarding new religious movements that the deprogrammers won this press war. After all, if *your* children were recruited by a wacko cult, persuaded to hand over all their possessions, then sent out on to the streets to sell shoddy products for twenty hours a day without rest, proper food or shelter, wouldn't *you* do everything in your power to get them out? So successful were the deprogrammers at the start of Ted Patrick's crusade that even when the police were alerted to ongoing kidnappings by the screams of the victims they frequently looked the other way. In at least one case, when a devotee actually managed to escape his kidnappers and fled to the police seeking protection, they put him into a squad car and returned him to Patrick for more treatment.

This attitude did not last. For many people, the kidnapping and incarceration of young Americans to remove their chosen religious beliefs was deeply unsettling. In 1973 a *Time* magazine feature likened deprogramming to the horrific 'brain-blowing' Ludovico technique used on Alex, the hero of [author] Anthony Burgess's *A Clockwork Orange*. Ethically, the issue was fraught with problems, and it wasn't long before it became obvious that kidnapping people because you didn't agree with their religious beliefs was illegal. Although he always made sure that at least one parent of the child concerned was present throughout his operations, it wasn't much longer before Ted Patrick was serving time for kidnapping.

Having realised that he was fallible, the Unification Church and other religious movements began to follow up the issue with lawyers. Kidnapping by parents—even if well intentioned—could not be condoned. And once deprogrammers such as Patrick had been sent to jail for their antics, it was easy to portray them as criminals. The ensuing legal battles between new religious groups and the various different incarnations of the Citizens Freedom Foundation [CFF, the predecessor to today's Cult Awareness Network] continue to this day, and have become extraordinarily acrimonious.

| "Those of us from a cult background be-
lieve in using our past to advance the
common good."

Some Ex-Cult Members
Maintain Healthy Connections
with Their Former Cults

Gina Catena

*In the following viewpoint, Gina Catena claims that people who
have left cults into which they were born, or second-generation
adults (SGAs), may continue to have relationships and be emotionally connected with members of the families and communities they left. Many experts, she believes, fail to accept that such
conflicting loyalties can exist among ex-cult members, and cults
can affect families for generations. Additionally, the adult children of SGAs may feel divided between their cult and post-cult
lives, states Catena, and need explanations on the limitations of
the cult lifestyle. The author is an ex-member of the Transcendental Meditation movement and is a member of the International Cultic Studies Association (ICSA).*

As you read, consider the following questions:

1. How does the author characterize the relationships between ex-cult members and their cult-based families?

Gina Catena, "Cult Is as Cult Does—Post Conference and Third-Generation Thoughts,"
ICSA Today, vol. 2, 2011. Reproduced by permission of the author.

2. How does Susan feel about her father's wife who is close to her own age, as told by Catena?

3. In what ways does the author say she attempts to reconcile her family's cult past with her children?

Over the years, a few attendees have impressed upon ICSA [International Cultic Studies Association] and cult experts that those raised in cults have different issues than do former cultists who joined and left. After all, those of us raised in cults lack a "precult identity" to which we can return after we leave a totalitarian ideology. Thankfully, ICSA now offers special recovery workshops and conference tracks for second-generation adults (SGAs).

Now to my personal highlight of the conference—an in-depth conversation with a woman I'll call Susan. Susan and I initially met a few years ago, over dinner at an earlier ICSA conference. Once again, we found ourselves sitting together at dinner on July 4th, 2010. Cult is as cult does, beyond the façade. We know that. Yet, it was still surprising for both Susan and me to learn that there are many similarities in our current lives as we casually chatted over a fabulous multi-course meal, fireworks, and New York City's skyline reflected on the nighttime river.

Susan was raised in a polygamist group in the Midwest. Like me, she left the group with her children, obtained an education and career. Her children are now self-supporting. She remains single.

Susan was raised with the small-town support of large families. Everyone dressed simply and worked hard, with an agricultural and manual labor–based economy. When Susan was 12 years old, her father took another wife, who was 14. A strict interpretation of Christian and Mormon scripture provided their overriding life guidance.

I was raised in a global setting that eventually settled into small-town Iowa, with a Hinduesque flavor; devout women wore sarees, and men had assigned colors for their suits. Many were employed outside the cult. Celibacy was the highest calling for the spiritually devout. Our daily routine had strict rules. Guidelines about diet, clothing, sleeping, and even architecture developed over time. Occult-esoteric spiritual beliefs guided life decisions. Many lived physically away from the group in which I was raised, but remained governed by Maharishi's [referring to Maharishi Mahesh Yogi, founder of Transcendental Meditation (TM)] occult dictates. Years after my children and I left, I also, remain single.

Larger Communities Are Complacent

Both of our groups support a spiritual hierarchy with peer pressure for ritualized practices. The economic basis of towns that surround our respective groups is dependent upon the groups' contribution to the larger local economy. As Susan said,

> Local law enforcement and others won't interfere with polygamist society because the outsiders are economically dependent upon the contributions from polygamist groups. Many of the sheriffs attended school with the polygamist men. They are old friends and won't interfere. There have been mixed marriages between those raised in polygamy and outsiders. No one will address the problems directly. The entire larger community is complacent with the polygamist lifestyle.

I concurred, saying,

> The same situation exists with Fairfield, Iowa. Even the current town mayor is "Governor of the Age of the Enlightenment"; his son had been arrested with a group of other TM-raised kids in a huge, illegal, marijuana-growing operation after the kids moved to California. The TM mayor does a good job managing the town. But the Transcendental Meditation group believes that its meditation reduces crime, so

the community avoids fully addressing certain situations as members arise to find practical solutions for the future. There are long-standing friendships between locals and TMers, shared community projects, and some intermarriages. Locals are reticent to publicly address misrepresentations, damaged psyches, or financial deceptions inherent in the TM movement's programs.

The lagging economy of Fairfield, Iowa, was revived through the influx of, and remains dependent upon, Maharishi's followers.

While the larger communities surrounding both our groups are well aware of various child neglect and repressed activities, economic dependency and fear of social stigma halt intervention.

Critical thinkers from both of our communities who can no longer tolerate the larger dysfunction usually relocate to create lives elsewhere. Both cult mentality and the surrounding mixed-cult mentality repress free expression and political activism. We suspect this must be common with communities adjacent to other sect groups.

Mixed Allegiances

Susan and I both gave birth at home within our respective groups. We both had been raised with a generalized distrust of the medical profession. We both left with our children; the oldest child was ten years old when we left. We both raised our children largely away from group dictates and social support. We both went deeply into debt to obtain education while working and raising children on our own. We'll probably never fully catch up financially. We both made blunders as we learned to function socially and professionally without background training. We both made it!

We both love many people from our cult-based families. We recognize their good intentions and naive devotion, while we reject such restrictive lives for ourselves. Some loved ones from our past maintain contact; many reject us for leaving and even more so for publicly revealing the underbelly of our respective heritages.

We also discussed how many cult "experts" don't understand our mixed allegiances and the ongoing effects upon our daily lives. We cannot completely leave the groupthink in our past because our families continue to carry multigenerational effects.

We found that we are strong because of our choice to leave a seemingly secure and narrow worldview. Now we each conduct active personal and professional lives unrelated to our cult families.

We both have experienced intimate relationships that are threatened by our history. Having tried to deny the past, despite ongoing family influences, we both agree that it's not worth denying our past to maintain a relationship. If we pretend that the early decades of our lives never happened, then our identity is not whole. We've tried; it doesn't work. And thus we remain single.

Susan said,

> I love the 14-year-old my father married when I was 12. Not that I agree with that lifestyle, but she is part of my family. I recently ran into my ex-mother-in-law (still living in polygamy); she said she misses me and still loves me. That must have been hard for her. We were happy to see one another!

I explained my aging parents; my father died last year, still in fantasy-think. My father believed he must have been a terrible person in a past life, that his decades of crippling pain were punishment for past-life transgressions, not due to his stubborn refusal to obtain proper medical care. He spent thousands of dollars on Maharishi's various mystical treatments.

As the next of kin, Susan and I try to keep our elders safe despite the challenges of their fantasy-based realities. Yet we simultaneously keep an emotional distance to protect our own sanity.

The Third-Generation Effects

Susan and I discussed what we called the third-generation effects in our respective families. Our adult children are divided between their post-cult lives and influences from idealistic, well-intentioned, cult-think family members who accuse us: "Your mother is blaming others. She's not taking responsibility for her life." At the same time, we attempt to explain to our respective children the limiting effects from a cult lifestyle and beliefs.

Both Susan and I were the only family members who explained the awkward past to our children; we apologized for our contribution to continuing the legacies when we were still sorting our own psyches. We absorb justifiable anger from our adult children. We hold a family base and acknowledge the larger families' confusing mixed messages and our errors in judgment. We give as we can personally and professionally to prevent such future abuses. Our part-time activism seems to keep the wounds open for our adult children. We've learned to tread lightly on the topic at home, while using our history to help others. . . .

At the conference, we had similar conversations with others from around the world who cope with mixed cult influences on children. While ICSA and others in the cult-studies field begin to study and publish about SGAs, time marches onward. Many SGAs are now middle-aged and older. We brainstorm among ourselves how best to support our children, the third-generation adults. We try to provide straightforward communication about difficult topics. Another woman raised in polygamy told of her grown son's insight.

Out of the blue he said, "It will take several generations to get this out of our family, won't it?" Her son is correct. . . .

ICSA is a group, as any honest human group, with a common purpose. ICSA members rejoice in shared common purpose; we don't always agree. We share, discuss, agree to disagree, and then return to our private lives. Those of us from a cult background believe in using our past to advance the common good; for those of us who live with ongoing cross-cultural influences, connecting and learning.

> "Now it seemed that the only children
> ever kept safe after leaving the cult were
> the ones we helped to go underground."

Children Should Not Be Returned to Their Parents in Cults

Flora Jessop and Paul T. Brown

Flora Jessop is a former member of the Fundamentalist Church of Jesus Christ of Latter-day Saints (FLDS) and an anti-polygamy activist. She co-wrote Church of Lies *with Paul T. Brown, an author and photographer. In the following viewpoint excerpted from* Church of Lies, *Jessop argues that the return of children to polygamist groups is a failure of the child welfare system. She accuses the FLDS of not only facilitating underage marriages, but sexually and physically abusing girls and boys that were removed from the Yearning for Zion Ranch in 2008. Despite the overwhelming physical evidence, however, Texas Child Protective Services (CPS) violated its own policies and sent the children back to the abusive homes of the cult, Jessop claims.*

Flora Jessop, Paul T. Brown, *Church of Lies*, Hoboken, NJ: Jossey-Bass, 2009. This material is used by permission of John Wiley & Sons, Inc.

As you read, consider the following questions:

1. What evidence of physical and sexual abuse of YFZ children does Jessop provide?

2. Why were YFZ children returned to their parents, according to Jessop?

3. How did the system fail women of the FLDS, as stated by Jessop?

Ever since I left my home in the Fundamentalist Church of Jesus Christ of Latter-day Saints (FLDS) compound in the twin cities of Hildale, Utah, and Colorado City, Arizona, and started telling the truth about my life in the FLDS, people have always said the same damn thing: "You're making this stuff up."

But from the time *Church of Lies* was first published, a whole lot has happened to open people's eyes to what's really going on: the truth told in my book and in other books written by former FLDS members; the arrest, trial, and conviction of FLDS "Prophet" Warren Jeffs; the legal wrangling over the FLDS's wealthy United Effort Plan (UEP) Trust; and the infamous raid (and subsequent bungling by government authorities) on the cult's Yearning for Zion (YFZ) Ranch in Eldorado, Texas. It's a wriggling can of worms that everyone can see for themselves if they just open their eyes and look.

See for yourself what's happened since *Church of Lies* was first published.

Warren Jeffs Is Still in Jail, and Charged with More Crimes

Former FLDS "Prophet" Warren Jeffs was convicted in Utah of being an accomplice to rape. In November 2009, the Utah Supreme Court is scheduled to hear arguments in an appeal of Jeffs' 2007 criminal conviction. His attorneys allege improper jury instructions, the replacement of a juror after deliberations began, and insufficient evidence for conviction on both counts. Jeffs' attorneys are making a mockery of victims' rights. [The court ordered a new trial in July 2010.] They found a cash cow, and they're milking it for all it's worth with frivolous motions and BS pleadings—going so far as to try to get a judge in Arizona to make a ruling on law officer actions in Texas. Arrogant? I'd say so.

Warren Jeffs is currently in jail in Arizona, awaiting trial for ordering and performing underage marriages. Recently, he went on a hunger strike and jail staff had to force-feed him through a feeding tube. Why did they bother? Well, one staff member put it this way: "He's got a judge and jury to speak to." My sentiments exactly.

And there's more in store for Warren. As a consequence of the YFZ raid, Warren—along with YFZ's leader, Merril Jessop, and ten other FLDS men—now faces twenty-six additional criminal indictments related to sexual assaults, polygamy, and various other charges for the abuse of underage girls. Stay tuned to learn just how sickening the abuses were.

The UEP Trust Is Back in the News

Back in 2004, a court-appointed fiduciary was put in charge of the FLDS's United Effort Plan [UEP] Trust—which is worth about $114 million and owns most of the real property within the boundaries of Hildale and Colorado City. The cult backed off when the courts got involved. But after the state of Texas gave the children rescued from the YFZ Ranch back to the cult members on the ranch, the FLDS felt powerful again and began negotiating with Utah attorney general Mark Shurtleff to get the trust back. They were demanding that everyone who was not one of the FLDS faithful be kicked out of the twin towns and that even the public streets be deeded over to them. Their intent was to create a compound like the YFZ Ranch on the Utah-Arizona border.

But in August 2009, a Salt Lake City judge said that the FLDS had no standing in regard to a beneficiary trust. She ordered the FLDS to sell 400 acres of trust land in northern Arizona to pay off some of its $3 million in debts. This was a huge win for ex-FLDS members who were still living in their homes on UEP Trust property. Of course, the FLDS has appealed the ruling, so stay tuned on this one too. [The appeal was denied in November 2009.]

The Raid on Yearning for Zion Ranch in Texas

In April 2008, a joint Child Protective Services (CPS) and police intervention raid on the YFZ Ranch, in Eldorado, Texas, freed 439 children and some of their mothers. Splashed across the world media, this action helped open the eyes of the world to some of the truth about what was going on. It could have been salvation for the children who were freed . . . but once again, corruption and politics took over and the system failed.

Due to confidentiality issues, local Texas CPS workers and Texas rangers could not come forward and dispute the propaganda being spread by those Care Bear–colored FLDS mommies on the news, part of the well-oiled FLDS PR [public relations] machine.

But I can.

How the System Failed the Children

In June 2009, I spent a month traveling around Texas and visiting many of the facilities that housed the freed children. I spoke with caretakers, CPS workers, Texas rangers, and many others. One foster family told me the following: Twelve children—ranging in age from thirteen to four—were placed in their care for three months. Ten of the twelve had been victims of sexual abuse. Three young boys had such severe rectal damage they had no bowel control. A thirteen-year-old girl had already had a child, but her child was never located. A five-year-old boy had already suffered from *nineteen* broken bones. Now imagine those abuses times 439.

I learned that a special team had been sent from Austin, Texas, to close *all* of the FLDS cases and send children home, no matter what abuse a child had suffered. The special team says it was safe for those children to go home. Why? Because their mothers completed a two-hour parenting class and signed a paper saying they now understood what abuse was.

Local CPS workers who tried to get protection for these children were told to back down and were ordered not to do the job they were mandated to do. CPS workers told me, with tears in their eyes, how they literally had to push some of the children across the room, begging not to be returned to the cult, when they were ordered to return to the FLDS compound. Actions were taken that violated every CPS policy in returning these kids. Several attorneys quit the Texas CPS, stating they would not have their names connected to this systemic failure.

While I was in Texas only *one* of the original 439 freed children was still under CPS supervision—and that was terminated when the child, who had been forced into sexual slavery to Warren Jeffs at age twelve, was sent back to Utah to be fostered with a faithful FLDS family.

How the System Failed the Women

Several women wanted to leave YFZ when the children were first taken by the state. But because they didn't trust the government agencies to protect them on the outside, they waited to make sure that the protection was really there. As a result of the betrayal by government authorities, all those who had wanted out of the cult have now faded back in, knowing that they will not be protected if they leave.

I am also saddened, frustrated, and heartbroken because those YFZ women who were *not* innocent victims—those same Care Bear–colored mothers who sat and could not even cry while begging on TV for their children to be returned—were not held accountable. Until they are, the cycle will never be broken.

Polygamy in America

Incredibly, or maybe predictably, polygamy in America is still going strong, despite the fact that it's been illegal for a long, long time. Utah attorney general Mark Shurtleff has decided to run for the United States Senate. [Shurtleff ended his campaign.] At a meeting in Salt Lake City in August 2009, he implied that if elected, he will sponsor legislation to decriminalize polygamy. Wait a minute—as Utah's top cop, isn't it his job to prosecute felonies, not make the crime legal?

I met with a contact at the Arizona attorney general's office just before I went to Texas. I was told that after being given a list of all those living on the YFZ compound, this office found that virtually all of them had been collecting welfare benefits from Arizona (and possibly Utah) for the entire time they lived in Texas. Incredibly, Arizona plans *no* prosecutions for welfare fraud. Sounds to me like Arizona wanted them gone and financed the expansion of the FLDS into Texas. Anyone else would have been prosecuted. But we have seen over and over again that if you are a polygamist in America, you are not held to the same laws as the rest of us.

Fighting On

The YFZ women weren't the only ones to feel betrayed by how the raid on the ranch was handled. Ex-FLDS members who have spent years trying to get help for their families still inside the cult had their hearts ripped to shreds when Texas sent all of the kids back. Due to this massive setback, almost all the ex-FLDS activists and advocates have quit their efforts and gone silent, feeling they have nowhere to turn to help those they left behind.

After I returned home from Texas, I found that not only my heart but also my soul was shattered. I have been fighting for abused children for close to twenty years. Now it seemed that the only children ever kept safe after leaving the cult were the ones we helped to go underground and out of the CPS and court system. Pretty sad. Since the first government raid on the FLDS—that 1953 raid on Short Creek, whose story was the cautionary tale of my childhood—I feel that not one single child has been truly protected through the child protection system. If nineteen broken bones are not enough, how many does it take before a five-year-old can live in a home where he feels safe?

I needed to feel safe too. As I do periodically, I went off the grid for a while to recharge my batteries, before I burned out. I needed to reconnect to life; to find hope, faith, and trust again. For now, I'm enjoying time with friends and family, and they've helped me to sort out the horror and pain of knowing that so many were failed. Spirited and true young people, like my daughter, Shauna, and my friend Ila Ferguson's grandson Steven, have really helped with that. I'm taking time to smell the roses and watch the sunsets, and to find peace on this journey called life.

To be honest, this time I was not sure I would be able to come back and fight again. But I did come back, and I am not backing down. I am coming back to fight even harder for the justice due to every victim of polygamy enslavement. I'm going to continue fighting for the women and children whose lives have been crippled by polygamy. Mostly, though, I will give my voice to every child who has the courage to seek help. When a child calls for help, whether inside or outside polygamy, I will drop what I am doing and give every last ounce of myself to help that child in his or her search for safety and freedom. And I won't stop until they are all living free.

Periodical and Internet Sources Bibliography

The following articles have been selected to supplement the diverse views presented in this chapter.

Miguel Bustillo — "Former Polygamist Is Thorn in Sect's Side," *Los Angeles Times*, June 30, 2008.

Ed Caesar — "The British Waco Survivors," *Sunday Times* (United Kingdom), December 14, 2008.

Jack Coraggio — "A Writer in Bridgewater Found Way Out of Cult," *Litchfield County Times* (Connecticut), July 10, 2008.

Eliott C. McLaughlin — "Ex-Sect Members Escape Polygamy but Not Pain," CNN, April 16, 2008. http://articles.cnn.com.

Patrick O'Reilly — "Psychotherapy with Former Cult Members," Psychotherapy.net, 2011. www.psychotherapy.net.

Michelle Roberts — "Abuse Survivors Struggle with Loss of Faith, Confidence," *Baptist Standard* (Texas), November 7, 2008.

Patrice St. Germain — "Escaping a Lifestyle," *Spectrum* (Utah), May 11, 2007.

Joseph Szimhart — "Razor's Edge Indeed: A Deprogrammer's View of Harmful Cult Activity," *Cultic Studies Review*, vol. 8, no. 3, 2009.

Jayanti Tamm — "Leaving a Cult," *On Faith*, April 3, 2009. http://onfaith.washingtonpost.com.

For Further Discussion

Chapter 1

1. Jayanti Tamm warns that cults are dangerous, unhealthy groups that must be recognized. On the other hand, Douglas E. Cowan and David G. Bromley insist that the term "cult" is often used inaccurately to describe harmless new religious movements. In your opinion, who provides the most compelling argument? Use examples from the viewpoints to explain your answer.

2. Brad Hirschfield proposes that all religions, at one point, exhibited the traits of a cult. Do you agree or disagree with the author? Why or why not?

3. Christopher Hitchens alleges that Mormonism is a religion based on sinister beliefs. In your view, does Michael Riley successfully counter such claims? Cite examples from the texts to support your response.

4. Supporting its potential as a religion, Janet Reitman urges the Church of Scientology to address the controversial treatment of its members. In your opinion, does this acknowledgement give Amy Scobee's position more validity than Reitman's? Why or why not?

Chapter 2

1. Bruce A. Robinson insists that most harmful religious groups are Christian and are ignored by anticult activists. In your view, does Tom O'Connor ignore these groups? Choose examples from the viewpoints to illustrate your position.

2. Jacob Hodgen proclaims that polygamy is a practical approach to building families, and Mormons must embrace their polygamist origins. Do you agree or disagree with the author? Why or why not?

Chapter 3

1. Michael Haag claims that brainwashing may be used by cults to coerce members into submission to perform harmful acts. Bruce A. Robinson, however, asserts that psychological means cannot produce mind control. In your opinion, who offers the most persuasive argument? Cite examples from the texts to explain your response.

2. Robin Jackson describes four reasons people join cults— intellectual, emotional, social, and spiritual. In your view, which is the most influential reason, and why?

Chapter 4

1. Dominic Streatfeild maintains that cult deprogrammers have employed a variety of tactics that harmed members or were counterproductive. In your view, does Rick Alan Ross promote or condone harmful tactics to remove individuals from cults? Use examples from the viewpoints to support your answer.

2. Flora Jessop and Paul T. Brown argue for removing children from their families in cults. In your opinion, do they provide enough evidence to support their view? Choose examples from the text to explain your response.

Organizations to Contact

The editors have compiled the following list of organizations concerned with the issues debated in this book. The descriptions are derived from materials provided by the organizations. All have publications or information available for interested readers. The list was compiled on the date of publication of the present volume; the information provided here may change. Be aware that many organizations take several weeks or longer to respond to inquiries, so allow as much time as possible.

American Academy of Religion (AAR)
825 Houston Mill Road NE, Suite 300
Atlanta, GA   30329-4205
(404) 727-3049 • fax: (404) 727-7959
website: www.aarweb.org

The American Academy of Religion (AAR) is an association of academic professionals dedicated to "fostering excellence in the study of religion." Founded in 1909, the academy publishes *Journal of the AAR, Religious Studies News*, and numerous books and other periodicals. Archives of articles and press releases can be found on its website.

Center for Studies on New Religions (CESNUR)
Via Confienza 19, Torino   10121
  Italy
+39-011-541950 • fax: +39-011-541905
website: www.cesnur.org

The Center for Studies on New Religions (CESNUR) is an international network of scholarly associations working in the field of new religious movements; the main headquarters is in Torino, Italy. Established in 1988, the network is dedicated to providing accurate information about various esoteric and spiritual movements and to countering propaganda from both cults and anticult groups. CESNUR also guides former cult members to helpful resources. The website, published in Italian with English translations available for most sections, offers numerous resources, including the center's library catalog of more than twenty thousand volumes. Topics range from New Age to mainstream religion to occult-related popular culture.

Cult Awareness Network (CAN)

3055 Wilshire Boulevard, Suite 900, Los Angeles, CA   90010
e-mail: can@cultawarenessnetwork.org
website: www.cultawarenessnetwork.org

The present-day Cult Awareness Network (CAN) is an organization owned by associates of the Church of Scientology that is dedicated to distributing information on religious movements and promoting peaceful religious debate. The original CAN was founded in 1978 as the Citizens Freedom Foundation (CFF), which aimed to educate the public on alleged cult brainwashing and to help former cult members readjust to society. The organization adopted the name Cult Awareness Network in the mid-1980s, but its involvement in deprogramming and other controversial practices brought about a series of lawsuits, many of which were initiated by the Church of Scientology, which caused CAN to declare bankruptcy years later; the current owners of CAN subsequently bought its assets at auction. The current CAN website provides numerous articles and links to information on various religions as well as criticism of its predecessor organization and other cult opponents.

Freedom of Mind Resource Center

716 Beacon Street, #590443, Newton, MA   02459
(617) 396-4638 • fax: (617) 628-8153
website: www.freedomofmind.com

Freedom of Mind Resource Center, operated by anticult activist and counselor Steven Hassan, is dedicated to "combating cult mind control" (the title of Hassan's best-known book) and easing former cult members' readjustment to mainstream society. The center also works to educate the public on the dangers of cults; its website provides a recommended reading list as well as numerous other resources for former cult members and the general public.

Hartford Institute for Religion Research
Hartford Seminary, 77 Sherman Street
Hartford, CT   06105-2260
(860) 509-9542 • fax: (860) 509-9551
e-mail: hirr@hartsem.edu
website: http://hirr.hartsem.edu

The Hartford Institute for Religion Research is "committed to providing quality . . . scientific religion research information that is helpful for religious leaders and the general public." Its website includes a section on new religious movements and provides links to relevant sites and an extensive collection of articles.

Inform
Houghton Street, London   WC2A 2AE
   England
+44 (0)20 7955 7654
website: http://inform.ac

Inform is an independent charity founded in 1988 and based at the London School of Economics. Its purpose is to provide objective and accurate information on new and alternative religious movements. Its website provides leaflets, publications, and information on cults and minority religions, as well as guidelines for friends and families of cult members.

International Cultic Studies Association (ICSA)
PO Box 2265, Bonita Springs, FL   34133
(239) 514-3081 • fax: (305) 393-8193
e-mail: mail@icsamail.com
website: www.icsahome.com

The International Cultic Studies Association (ICSA) is an interdisciplinary network of academicians, former cult members, and other interested parties dedicated to educating the public on authoritarian tactics and zealotry as expressed in alternative religious movements and similar groups. Founded in 1979 as the American Family Foundation (AFF), ICSA adopted its current name in 2004 as better suiting an increasingly international and scholarly focus. Its website provides access to archives of *Cultic Studies Review* and *Cult Studies Journal*, along with an online bookstore, information service, and calendar of events.

Ontario Consultants on Religious Tolerance (OCRT)
PO Box 27026, Kingston, ON
  K7M 8W5
  Canada
e-mail: ocrtfeedback@gmail.com
website: www.religioustolerance.org

The Ontario Consultants on Religious Tolerance (OCRT) is a Canada-based agency dedicated to promoting individual religious freedom by distributing accurate information, debating false information, and discussing hot topics in current religious debate. The organization strives to present information from as many points of view as possible. Its website presents essays on numerous religions and other topics, along with a discussion forum and a list of recommended reading.

Reasoning from the Scriptures Ministries
PO Box 5668, Frisco, TX   75035
(214) 618-0912
e-mail: ronrhodes@earthlink.net
website: http://ronrhodes.org

Reasoning from the Scriptures Ministries is a Christian organization dedicated to countering the claims of cults and other non-Christian religions through apologetic debate. The ministry puts out a bimonthly e-publication with subscriptions available through its website, which also features an online bookstore and large library of links to related web content.

Rick A. Ross Institute
1977 N. Olden Avenue, Ext #272, Trenton, NJ   08618
(609) 396-6684 • fax: (609) 964-1842

e-mail: info@rickross.com
website: www.rickross.com

The Rick A. Ross Institute is a nonprofit organization dedicated to research and public education of the topic of "destructive cults" and controversial religious movements. Its website provides extensive resources and links for researchers, former cult members, and the public, including an Open Forum page.

Watchman Fellowship
PO Box 13340, Arlington, TX   76094
(817) 277-0023 • fax: (817) 277-8098
website: www.watchman.org

The Watchman Fellowship is "a ministry of Christian discernment" that aims to evaluate new religious movements and the occult from a Christian perspective. Founded in 1979, the organization now has several offices in the United States. Its website offers a "Resource Catalog" on cults, new religious movements, and major religions, as well as a free newsletter subscription.

Berthoud Community
Library District
236 Welch Ave
(970) 532 2757

Bibliography of Books

Raphael Aron — *Cults, Terror, and Mind Control.* Pt. Richmond, CA: Bay Tree Publishing, 2009.

Lee B. Baker — *Mormonism: A Life Under False Pretenses.* Sarasota, FL: First Edition Design Publishing, 2012.

Sanjiv Bhattacharya — *Secrets and Wives: The Hidden World of Mormon Polygamy.* Berkeley, CA: Counterpoint, 2011.

Bruce Bickel and Stan Jantz — *World Religions and Cults 101: A Guide to Spiritual Beliefs.* Eugene, OR: Harvest House Publishers, 2005.

Lorne L. Dawson — *Comprehending Cults: The Sociology of New Religious Movements.* New York: Oxford University Press, 2006.

David Frankfurter — *Evil Incarnate: Rumors of Demonic Conspiracy and Ritual Abuse in History.* Princeton, NJ: Princeton University Press, 2006.

Arthur Goldwag — *Cults, Conspiracies, and Secret Societies: The Straight Scoop on Freemasons, the Illuminati, Skull and Bones, Black Helicopters, the New World Order, and Many, Many More.* New York: Vintage Books, 2009.

J.C. Hallman — *The Devil Is a Gentleman: Exploring America's Religious Fringe.* New York: Random House, 2006.

Brenda Lee — *Out of the Cocoon: A Young Woman's Courageous Flight from the Grip of a Religious Cult.* Bandon, OR: Robert D. Reed Publishers, 2006.

Candy Gwen Lopitz — *Spiritual Battery.* Maitland, FL: Xulon Press, 2011.

Henry Makow — *Illuminati: The Cult That Hijacked the World.* Winnipeg, Canada: Silas Green, 2011.

Chris Mikul — *Cult Files—True Stories from the Extreme Edges of Religious Belief.* New York: Metro Books, 2010.

Larry A. Nichols, George A. Mather, and Alvin J. Schmidt — *Encyclopedic Dictionary of Cults, Sects, and World Religions.* Grand Rapids, MI: Zondervan, 2006.

Tim Reiterman — *Raven: The Untold Story of the Rev. Jim Jones and His People.* New York: J.P. Tarcher/Penguin, 2008.

Janet Reitman — *Inside Scientology: The Story of America's Most Secretive Religion.* Boston, MA: Houghton Mifflin Harcourt, 2011.

Julie Scheeres — *A Thousand Lives: The Untold Story of Hope, Deception, and Survival at Jonestown.* New York: Free Press, 2011.

Margaret Thaler Singer — *Cults in Our Midst: The Continuing Fight Against Their Hidden Menace.* San Francisco, CA: Jossey-Bass, 2003.

Robert L. Snow   *Deadly Cults: The Crimes of True
                    Believers.* Westport, CT: Praeger,
                    2003.

Irene Spencer   *Cult Insanity: A Memoir of Polygamy,
                    Prophets, and Blood Atonement.* New
                    York: Center Street, 2009.

Jayanti Tamm   *Cartwheels in a Sari: A Memoir of
                    Growing Up Cult.* New York:
                    Harmony Books, 2009.

Eldon Taylor   *Mind Programming: From Persuasion
                    and Brainwashing to Self-Help and
                    Practical Metaphysics.* Carlsbad, CA:
                    Hay House, 2009.

Kathleen Taylor   *Brainwashing: The Science of Thought
                    Control.* New York: Oxford University
                    Press, 2004.

Kim Taylor   *Daughters of Zion: A Family's
                    Conversion to Polygamy.* Grants Pass,
                    OR: Rogue Hill Publishing, 2008.

Jack B. Worthy   *The Mormon Cult: A Former
                    Missionary Reveals the Secrets of
                    Mormon Mind Control.* Tucson, AZ:
                    See Sharp Press, 2008.

Index

A

Absolute control by cults, 23–24
Absolute truth claims, 82
Abuse
    domestic abuse, 131
    by polygamist cults, 112–114
    religion-related, 89
    by religious cult movements,
     40
    ritual abuse, 85, 90, 141
    See also Child abuse; Sexual
     abuse
ACM. *See* Anticult movement
  (ACM)
After Jesus Dies (Duncan), 16
Agnosticism, 72
Agreeableness trait, 152–154
al Qaeda ideology, 132
Alexander, Joe, 178
Alger, Fanny, 120–121
Allport, Gordon, 151, 152–153
Alternative religious movements,
  33, 85
Ambivert trait, 154
American Civil Liberties Union
  (ACLU), 120
American Cult Awareness Net-
  work, 156–157
American Family Foundation, 30
American Psychiatric Association,
  152
American Psychological Associa-
  tion (APA), 129, 144
American Sociological Association,
  143

Anderson, Larry, 65
Answers in Action, 145
Anti-Catholic prejudice, 57
Anti-polygamy laws, 112, 116–117
Anticult activism, 29, 166–167
Anticult movement (ACM)
    brainwashing beliefs, 30, 86,
     139–142
    kidnapping by, 138
    mind control and, 139–140
    new religious movements and,
     138–142
APA Monitor (magazine), 144
Apocalyptic thinking
  (eschatology), 15, 41–42, 81
Armageddon, 14, 19, 52
Armed forces training units, 31
Association for World Academics
  for Religious Education
  (AWARE), 147–148
Audience cults, 81
Aum Shinrikyo, 79, 132
Awake! publication, 19

B

Bachmann, Michele, 57
Baird, Al, 126–127
Baptist Church, 50, 52, 54
Barker, Eileen, 146
Beck, Glenn, 51
Beckford, James, 30
Beghe, Jason, 65
Belief coercion, 87–89
Belief systems
    absolute truth claims, 82